WHO IS A SIKH?

Who is a Sikh?

The Problem of Sikh Identity

W. H. McLeod

CLARENDON PRESS · OXFORD

Oxford University Press, Walton Street, Oxford OX2 6DP
Oxford New York Toronto
Delhi Bombay Calcutta Madras Karachi
Petaling Jaya Singapore Hong Kong Tokyo
Nairobi Dar es Salaam Cape Town
Melbourne Auckland
and associated companies in
Berlin Ibadan

Oxford is a trade mark of Oxford University Press

Published in the United States
by Oxford University Press, New York

British Library Cataloguing in Publication Data
McLeod, W. H. (William Hewat), 1932–
Who is a Sikh.
1. Sikh life
I. Title
294.6'44
ISBN 0–19–826548–4

Library of Congress Cataloging in Publication Data
McLeod, W. H.
Who is a Sikh: the problem of Sikh identity
W. H. McLeod.
1. Sikhs. 2. Sikhism. I. Title.
BL2018.M319 1989 294.6—dc19 89-2936
ISBN 0–19–826548–4

Printed in Great Britain by
Biddles Ltd., Guildford and King's Lynn

PREFACE

THIS book consists of lectures which could not be given. The Trustees of the Radhakrishnan Memorial Bequest had invited me to visit the University of Oxford and give the series for 1986–7. Dates had been arranged for March 1987, the six lectures had been duly written, and I was due to depart for Oxford in one month. It was then that the illness occurred which put an end to such plans. I had hoped that with rapid progress I would be ready to deliver them a year later than intended, but that also proved to be too optimistic. New Zealand was too far from England and eventually it was decided, with much reluctance, that the Radhakrishnan Memorial Lectures for 1986–7 would have to be cancelled.

The series had, however, been written and it was decided that even if they could not be heard it was at least possible that they could be read. It was unfortunate that they could not be presented before the members of an Oxford audience in order that due attention could be paid to their criticisms before publication. Such an advantage was not to be and it was felt that even in their uncriticized form they would be preferable to no lectures at all.

Punjabi words have presented the usual difficulty of when to italicize and when to leave as roman. Words indicating various kinds of people and organizations have been allowed to remain roman. Punjabi words which occur frequently in English usage (e.g. mañjī, saṅgat) have been italicized the first time and then printed in roman thereafter. Other Punjabi words have been italicized and marked with diacriticals throughout. All have been included in the Glossary, complete with diacriticals.

Three universities (or their various parts) deserve my gratitude. The University of Otago granted me the leave which was necessary if I was to be removed from distractions and diversions. To it I express my thanks and in particular to my fellow-members of the History Department for making my absence possible. The Centre for Religious Studies at the University of Toronto provided me with the facilities, without duties or interruption, to write the lectures. It too deserves my thanks. Finally there are the Trustees of the Radhakrishnan Memorial Bequest for their generous invitation to visit the University of Oxford and deliver the lectures. In this I failed, but I remain profoundly indebted to them for having prompted me to produce a text. To them, and to the memory of Sarvapalli Radhakrishnan, I offer in sincere gratitude these thoughts on who is a Sikh.

H. M.

The University of Otago
Dunedin

CONTENTS

1

What is Sikhism?

'WHAT is Sikhism?' I asked a Sikh gentleman many years ago. 'How would you define it?'

'Sikhism', he replied, 'can be defined as the fatherhood of God and the brotherhood of man.'

The answer is a popular one and it is an interesting response for several reasons. One reason is that it so clearly evokes the memory of Adolf Harnack and his famous Berlin lectures published as *What is Christianity?*[1] My informant was quoting the words which conventionally summarize Harnack's book and which were so commonly used to describe the essence of Liberal Protestant belief. Sikhism is scarcely the same as Liberal Protestantism, but one can easily understand why the vague formula should exercise such an appeal. Dogma is discarded and friendly benevolence retained.

Although the Liberal Protestant creed must be rejected as an adequate definition for Sikhism, we should pause before we dismiss all such summary statements. Concise or mnemonic summaries have been extensively used in the Sikh tradition and one early example retains its popularity to the present day. The earliest of all goes back to Guru Nanak himself, a saying consisting of nothing more than the three nouns *nām*, *dān*, and *iśnān*.[2] The *nām dān iśnān* formula evidently served as a kind of motto for the early community, neatly expressing the essence of Nanak's message and easily remembered by those who acknowledged him as their Guru.

Nām, or the 'divine Name', is a convenient shorthand for the total being and nature of Akal Purakh or God, a single word which effectively captures a broad range of direct meaning and indirect association.[3] One

---

[1] Adolf Harnack, *What is Christianity?* (1st Eng. edn., Williams & Norgate, London, 1901). The lectures were delivered in the University of Berlin during 1899–1900.

[2] Guru Nanak, *Siddh Goṣṭ* 36, Adi Granth, p. 942. The formula is extensively used in sakhis of the Narrative III janam-sakhi tradition. W. H. McLeod, *The B40 Janam-sākhī* (Amritsar, 1980), 110n. It also appears in the *Tanakhāh-nāmā* attributed to Bhai Nand Lal. Piara Singh Padam (samp.), *Rahit-nāme* (Patiala, 1974), 44. See chap. 3, n. 31.

[3] W. H. McLeod, *Gurū Nānak and the Sikh Religion* (Oxford, 1968; 2nd edn., Delhi, 1976), 195–6.

might well argue that the expounding of this single word should tell us all that we need to know about the fundamental doctrine which Nanak preached. The two remaining words merely amplify its meaning. If one is to secure deliverance from the cycle of transmigration, one must accept the reality of the *nām* and strive to bring one's own being into complete conformity with it. This purpose one achieves primarily through the practice of *nām simaraṇ* or meditation on the divine Name, though it is also assisted by alms-giving (*dān*) and necessarily involves pure living (*iśnān*).

The strength of this earliest of formulas obviously resides in its first word and it soon becomes clear that an extended explanation is required before it can be clearly understood. It is, moreover, evident that much of the developed Sikh tradition is missing. The same verdict must be applied to another formula popularly (but mistakenly) attributed to Guru Nanak. *Nām japo, kirat karo, vaṇḍ chhako*, he is believed to have declared. 'Repeat the divine Name, work [hard], and give to others a portion of what you earn.'[4] The ideal is an admirable one. As with *nām dān iśnān*, however, it must leave us with the distinct impression that much of the Sikh tradition has somehow been missed. Where, for example, is the mandatory reference to the Khalsa or to the Rahit which all its members should observe?[5]

A standard rule to follow when seeking summary answers to questions concerning the Sikh tradition is to consult Kahn Singh Nabha's encyclopaedia *Guruśabad ratanākar mahān koś*. How does Kahn Singh define what he calls *sikh dharam*? Having briefly summarized Nanak's doctrine of God and stressed the paramount need for the Guru's guidance, he lists the following as essential articles of faith:

I. Individual
1. To achieve mystical union with God (*Vāhigurū*) through meditation on the divine Name.
2. To read the sacred scripture (*gurbāṇī*) daily and to reflect on the doctrines which it imparts.
3. To view all men as brothers without concern for caste or race, bestowing love on all and performing service without expectation of reward.

---

[4] The origin is obscure, though apparently relatively recent. Dr Ganda Singh suggests it may owe its beginnings to the phrase *jinān nām japiā, vaṇḍ chhakiā . . . di kamāi dā dhiān dhar ke*, which occurs in Ardas (the 'Sikh Prayer'). See chap. 7, n. 11. Personal letter 19 Nov. 1971.

[5] The Khalsa is the order instituted by Guru Gobind Singh in 1699, and its Rahit is the code of conduct which all who join it are expected to obey. See chap. 3.

4. To secure the benefits of religion (*dharam*) while continuing to live the life of an ordinary layman.
5. To spurn ignorant notions of untouchability, magic, idol worship, and superstition; and to accept only the teachings of the Guru.

II. Corporate
1. To observe the Sikh code of conduct (*rahit*) in the bonds of unity.
2. To accept the corporate community (*panth*) as Guru and to serve it with loyal devotion.
3. To proclaim the Guru's teachings to the world.
4. To accept with affection all Nanak-panthis as adherents of the Sikh religion, regardless of their outward appearance; and to treat people with respect and sympathy.
5. To observe in gurdwaras and other shrines the rituals enjoined by the Gurus.[6]

Kahn Singh was a master of the succinct statement and his skill is well represented by these Ten Commandments. In spite of their brevity they carry us a considerable distance, and, were we to examine each item in turn, we could reasonably expect to acquire a wide understanding of Sikh doctrine. The essential problem, however, remains. The Sikh tradition refuses to be thus encapsulated and a closer examination would certainly lead us into some major controversies. What, for example, is Kahn Singh telling us about the role and status of the Khalsa? The word does not appear in his catalogue although its presence is implied by his reference to the Rahit. A significant part of the answer is indicated by his reference to Nanak-panthis in item II. 4 and it is a view which some would certainly want to qualify.

The issue raised by this item concerns the difference between those who regard the Khalsa as the essential and definitive form of the Sikh tradition and those who affirm a broader identity. It is a fundamental issue which clearly signals the kind of problem which we expect to encounter as we endeavour to answer the question 'What is Sikhism?' Indeed some will maintain that no answer is possible until we abandon the term 'Sikhism' altogether. Amongst those who wish to retain the word there are some who hesitate to use it with reference to the early period of Sikh development, preferring to restrict its usage to the last three centuries. According to this latter view, the term 'Sikhism' should be reserved for that area of Sikh tradition which is amenable to clear definition, namely the Khalsa. Further complexity emerges when we discover that this restrictive view further subdivides, distinguishing those

---

[6] Kahn Singh Nabha, *Guruśabad ratanākar mahān koś* (2nd rev. edn., Patiala, 1960), 145.

who would accept non-Khalsa Sikhs as affiliates from those who would exclude them altogether.

Plainly we are running into difficulties and the time has come to indicate how we propose to deal with them. The only satisfactory method seems to be to treat the tradition historically. Observing how it emerges and grows, we should be able to comprehend something of the variety of doctrine and practice which develops within the tradition as its numbers increase and as changing pressures work upon it. In so doing we shall be led from the question 'What is Sikhism?' to the question 'Who is a Sikh?' The two issues differ, yet fundamentally they are the same. Most Sikhs (like most who identify with any of the major religious groupings) would have difficulty in recognizing much that is offered as an answer to the first question. They are nevertheless products of the tradition and of the history which has made it. Without the tradition they would be different people, identifying with a different tradition or with several.

We shall begin, predictably, with Guru Nanak and with the group of followers whom he attracted (the group which comes to be known as the Nanak-panth), exploring their beginnings and the pattern of development which was followed under the early Gurus. We shall proceed to examine the founding of the Khalsa by Guru Gobind Singh; and we shall then seek to follow the evolution of the Khalsa code of conduct (the Rahit) during the course of the eighteenth century. Another key period in the development of the Sikh identity, the decades occupied by the Singh Sabha and Akali movements, will then be considered. Answers to some crucial questions were given during the half-century from 1873 to 1925 and their effect has been to mould much that has taken place since then. Finally, we shall pose the question 'Who is a Sikh?', setting it in its modern context. In attempting to answer it we shall simultaneously endeavour to define the nature of Sikhism as it is generally understood today.

Although this procedure should help us to understand the Sikh tradition, let us not imagine that it will produce answers which are clear, definitive, and universally accepted. If that were our objective, we should assuredly fail, for Sikh identity cannot be described with the ease or clarity which so commonly we assume. Paradoxically it is the increasingly clear definition of Sikh identity which produces an increasingly acute problem of identity. When dealing with the Nanak-panth we may perhaps obtain some general definitions which apply to the tradition as a whole, but having reached the Khalsa we shall be confronted by a diversity of interpretations. As we have already noted, many Sikhs believe that the Khalsa definition and the distinctive Khalsa identity of today supply clear and immediate answers to all such questions. Others are less certain that the boundaries of the tradition can be drawn in a manner which effectively excludes those who claim to be Sikhs yet decline to observe the traditional code of the Khalsa.

This is one of the primary issues which awaits us and we mislead ourselves if we imagine that the debate covers only two distinct identities (the Khalsa and the non-Khalsa). The different between the punctilious Gursikh of the Khalsa and the so-called Sahaj-dhari Sikh may be clear enough, but what are we to make of those who observe much of the Khalsa discipline (particularly the uncut hair) without formally taking initiation?[7] Even more difficult are the questions implicitly raised by those who observe multiple identities, definable as neither clearly Hindu nor clearly Sikh. And how are we to classify those who belong to families which traditionally observe the Khalsa tradition yet cut their hair?

Amongst Sikhs living overseas the cutting of hair has long been a common practice, and, although recent events have slowed the process, there seems to be little doubt that the clearly established trend towards hair-cutting will continue. Such people still claim to be Sikhs. Are they mistaken, or should the boundaries of the Sikh tradition somehow be drawn in a manner which includes them? If they are to be included, what are we to make of the orthodox insistence on upholding the traditions of the Khalsa, and how should this latter variety of hair-cutting Sikh be compared with the Sahaj-dhari who has never kept his or her hair uncut?

It must be clearly recognized that a significant part of the problem derives from our typically Western insistence on clearly defined categories, on neatly labelled normative boxes into which all men and women should somehow be fitted. In this respect the problem is nevertheless the inevitable by-product of an essential process. We need the categories if analysis is to proceed; and we deceive ourselves only if we imagine that they can be arranged in a simple pattern.

A different kind of problem is raised by those who insist that the Sikh tradition can only be understood if we begin by acknowledging it to be an inalienable part of the larger Hindu tradition. It is futile to assert that this particular question need not be raised. Everyone knows (so it is claimed) that Nanak was a Hindu, and, although the Sikh tradition subsequently developed its own distinctive features, it remains firmly set within the

---

[7] A Gursikh of the Khalsa is a loyal Sikh of the Guru who, in obedience to the Khalsa rule, retains his or her hair uncut. A Sahaj-dhari is a Sikh who has never been a member of the Khalsa and has always cut his or her hair.

larger matrix of Hindu belief and social convention. This claim can be neither summarily accepted nor summarily dismissed, and the vehement assertions which it elicits are no substitute for patient analysis. For many Sikhs it is a very serious issue indeed, and if it is an important issue for them it must necessarily be an important issue for us also.

The problems are many and few of them will produce an agreed answer. The task is, however, worth undertaking, for in the process we can hope to draw nearer to that elusive consent. We begin at the beginning. What did it mean to be a Sikh of Guru Nanak in the early days of the community?

2

The Nanak-panth

NANAK was the first Guru of the Sikhs and his name requires no introduction. Everyone knows Guru Nanak, at least those who have the
vaguest interest in Sikh history or religion. 'Panth', however, requires a
preliminary definition. In its literal sense the word means 'path' or 'way'
and it has traditionally been used to designate the followers of a particular teacher or of a distinctive range of doctrine. The early followers of
Nanak thus constituted the Nanak-panth and came to be known as
Nanak-panthis as well as Sikhs or 'Learners'. Eventually, as the line of
Gurus lengthened and new ideals were introduced, Nanak's name was
dropped and Sikhs increasingly referred to themselves simply as the
Panth.

Panth is a word which yields no satisfactory English translation.
'Community' has been tainted in the Indian context by its association
with communalism, and 'sect' (as we shall later see) is also inappropriate.
The word has rich associations in Sikh usage and as such it is one which
deserves to be a part of standard English usage. In all that lies ahead in
this examination we shall respect that claim, referring only to the Panth
and never to the Sikh community.[1]

The person who attracted the original Nanak-panth was born in the
Punjab in 1469 and died there seventy years later. Nanak was a religious
teacher who gave uniquely clear and attractive expression to doctrines
and ideals which had developed within the Sant tradition of northern
India. The Sant tradition must be distinguished from the larger and more
diffuse Bhakti tradition with which it has generally been identified. The
reason for the confusion is easily recognized, for the Sants shared with the
Bhaktas a firm belief in the efficacy of personal devotion as the means to
securing deliverance from the cycle of transmigration. In other respects,
however, they diverge. The Sants would have nothing to do with incarna-
tions, idol worship, sacred scriptures, temples, or pilgrimages, at least not

---

[1] For an extended discussion, see W. H. McLeod, 'On the Word *panth*: A Problem of
Terminology and Definition', *Contributions to Indian Sociology*, 12/2 (1979), 287–95. See
also id., *The Evolution of the Sikh Community* (Oxford, 1976), 2–3.

in the external sense conventionally associated with such beliefs and practices. Because these were typically performed as exterior acts of piety, they were regarded by the Sants as worthless.

Devotion for the Sants was strictly an interior discipline, one which spurned all exterior custom and practice as a means to liberation. The emphasis was one which they shared with the yogic tradition of the Naths and the frequency of Nath terminology in basic Sant usage clearly points to Nath antecedents. This is not to suggest that the Sants should be closely associated with the Naths in terms of general sympathy or actual practice. On the contrary, as Nanak so insistently reminds us, the Sant could have no truck with the hatha-yoga of the Naths nor with their stress on harsh austerities. The Sants were ordinary people, propounding in their hymns an interior discipline which other ordinary people could practise without regard for inherited status or ascetic withdrawal from the world.[2]

The Sant message was a simple one and to many it must have seemed naïve. Such a judgement could never have been applied to the teachings which Nanak delivered. In his many hymns we find a highly sophisticated doctrine, yet one expressed in an eminently accessible form. Religious songs are not well suited to the promulgating of a systematic theology, but an analysis of his works can demonstrate that behind them lies an integrated pattern of belief and a clear conception of how that belief should be applied in practice.[3] Although they may create difficulties in terms of intellectual analysis, religious songs can be very effective as a means of communicating the elements of a faith and in regularly reinforcing it. These objectives were certainly achieved by Nanak's hymns (*bāṇī*) and those who followed him as his early successors built upon the foundation which he had so securely laid.

The teachings of Nanak and his early successors focused on the *nām* or divine Name, a term which we have already noted as the dominant feature of the popular *nām dān iśnān* formula. For all mankind the fundamental problem is the suffering imposed by the cycle of transmigration. *Nām* is the sure remedy offered by Akal Purakh, the 'Timeless One' who created the universe and lovingly watches over it. Akal Purakh, the Creator and Sustainer, dwells immanent in all creation and, because all that exists is an expression of the divine being, his creation represents the

[2] Charlotte Vaudeville, '*Sant Mat*: Santism as the Universal Path to Sanctity', in Karine Schomer and W. H. McLeod (eds.), *The Sants: Studies in a Devotional Tradition of India* (Berkeley and Delhi, 1987), 21–40.

[3] W. H. McLeod, *Gurū Nānak and the Sikh Religion* (Oxford, 1968; 2nd edn., Delhi, 1976), 148–50.

supreme manifestation of the *nām*. The *nām* is the ever-present and all-pervading presence of Akal Purakh, and whoever perceives this presence gains access to the means of mystical unity with Akal Purakh. In that condition of supreme peace lies salvation, for the person who attains it thereby achieves release from the baleful cycle of transmigration.

Although the *nām* is thus revealed for all to see and accept, men and women are congenitally blind, unable to perceive the truth which lies around and within each of them. Deceived by the mischievous prompting of their weak and wayward spirits, they are held in permanent subjection to evil passions and false beliefs. Vainly they seek the elusive means of deliverance, foolishly trusting in such external conventions as the temple, the mosque, devout ceremony, or a pious pilgrimage. None of these practices can achieve the end which they seek and those who preach them are agents of doom. Release can be found only by opening one's eyes to the *nām* and by appropriating its wonders within the mind and the heart.[4]

How then is each misguided person to perceive the *nām*, and how is it to be appropriated? Akal Purakh is gracious and to those who are willing to listen he speaks the word which reveals his truth. The 'voice' of Akal Purakh is the eternal *gurū* and the 'word' which the Guru utters is the *śabad*. It can be effectively 'heard' only by engaging in the practice of *nām simaraṇ* or 'remembrance of the Name'. This involves regular meditation, the focus of the meditation being the *nām*, which reveals around and within us the immanent presence of Akal Purakh. The essence of the *nām* is order and harmony. The objective of *nām simaraṇ* must be to achieve that same harmony and thus to merge one's spirit in the being of Akal Purakh.

For those who achieve this objective, two results will follow. One is the experience of ever-growing wonder (*visamād*), leading eventually to the rapturous peace of total blending in the divine (the condition which Nanak calls *sahaj*). The other is the final ending of the cycle of transmigration with its painful sequence of death and rebirth. Instead of earning the vile *karma* which follows from passion and evil deeds, one achieves instead that harmony which separates the spirit from all that keeps the cycle in motion. The end is peace, and with passions finally

---

[4] The term used to designate the inner faculty which determines a person's thought and actions, and which provides the arena for the discipline leading to release, is the *man*. In this explanation it is variously translated as 'spirit' and as 'heart'. There is in fact no adequate translation available in English, for *man* draws together the range of thought, emotion, and spiritual being which English variously distinguishes as 'mind', 'heart', and 'soul'. For a discussion of *man*, see ibid. 178–81, 220.

stilled one attains release. It is a condition which can be achieved during the present life, preceding the physical death which is its final seal. It is also a condition which can be achieved only within one's own inner being. External props and practices merely delude. In spiritual terms their effect must be fatal.[5]

This is the pattern of belief and practice which emerges from an exegesis of Nanak's works (his *bāṇī*). The same pattern informs the works of his first four successors and it thus constitutes the message of the Adi Granth (the scripture compiled by Guru Arjan in 1603–4). In a certain sense it can be regarded as the foundation and enduring core of the Sikh tradition and of the Panth which embodies that tradition. Although some of the later Gurus left no *bāṇī*, it is clearly evident from the works of the last two in the succession that the message of the divine Name was loyally sustained.[6] It is also evident that the message commands the same continuing loyalty within the modern Panth as we know it today.

This, however, is not the appropriate perspective from which to view the actual birth and subsequent development of the Panth. The Panth does indeed preserve and transmit a particular pattern of doctrine and devotional practice. It also consists of people, and those who constituted the early Nanak-panth need not have been fully aware of the specific theology which lay behind the songs of Nanak. This could never have been the case. The primary basis of the Nanak-panth will have been veneration for the particular teacher who revealed beauty in his compositions and piety in his way of life.

Veneration is the key to understanding the original formation of the Nanak-panth. The phenomenon is actually a common one, as a cursory survey of the modern scene in north India will so quickly show. Teachers appear and in attracting disciples they create minor panths. Most of them soon wane, surviving as small remnants or returning to the larger tradition from which they originally emerged. What we still need to explain is why this particular panth achieved such notable permanence. We must also endeavour to determine how much of the original Nanak inheritance was carried forward by the Nanak-panth and what features it developed during its subsequent period of growth.

The answer to the second of these questions must obviously lie ahead of us. To some extent the same also applies to the first question, for

---

[5] Ibid., chap. 5. Id. (trans.), *Textual Sources for the Study of Sikhism* (Manchester, 1984), section 3.1.1.

[6] McLeod (trans.), *Textual Sources for the Study of Sikhism*, pp. 46–53, 54–63.

permanence is not something which can be initially achieved and there-after taken for granted. There are, however, some important aspects of the answer which belong to the lifetime of Nanak himself and amongst these we must certainly include both the Guru's own reputation and the attractive quality of the hymns which he composed. To these we may also add a decision which he made, one which was plainly intended to ensure that the growing band of disciples and reverent admirers should not be permitted to dissolve after his death.

Before he died Nanak chose a successor, one who was to follow him as leader and guide of the Nanak-panth. The disciple chosen for this responsibility was Lahina, renamed Angad at the time of his selection.[7] A lineage was thus established and, although contending claimants were later to appear, a succession recognized as legitimate was maintained intact from the appointment of Guru Angad to the death of Guru Gobind Singh. It was a natural step to take, but not an inevitable one. Without a recognized succession the fledgling Nanak-panth could scarcely have survived, for there would have been no sufficient means of sustaining the loyalty of its adherents or their cohesion as an emergent tradition.

The Nanak-panth thus acquired a rudimentary organization, one which ensured a continuing existence beyond the lifetime of the first Guru. It was, however, too rudimentary for the strains which developed as the Panth grew older and its adherents increased in number. The appearance of later generations owing their adherence to birth rather than to personal choice imposes one variety of strain on a movement of this kind. Growing numbers impose another, particularly when there is a simultaneous expansion in geographical terms. To deal with these pressures a more developed form of panthic organization became increasingly necessary. There is considerable uncertainty with regard to the timing of the measures which were taken by Nanak's early successors, and indeed the actual measures themselves are not always clear. It seems that significant steps were taken during the time of Guru Amar Das (1552–74) and that the developments encouraged by these steps established the pattern of panthic organization which was to persist until the founding of the Khalsa at the end of the seventeenth century.[8]

The uncertainty associated with these developments should be stressed if we are to appreciate the shadowy nature of much that passes for historical fact during the period of the early Gurus. Measures which are traditionally associated with the period of Guru Amar Das and which

---

[7] J. S. Grewal, *Guru Nanak in History* (Chandigarh, 1969), 285–6.
[8] McLeod, *The Evolution of the Sikh Community*, pp. 7–10.

are viewed as the product of formal decisions may actually have longer pedigrees and less specific origins. Tradition is, however, reasonably firm on most of these points and, although our detailed understanding may be faulty, the eventual results seem beyond doubt. In these guarded terms we may attach to Guru Amar Das three distinct varieties of innovation. All three represent the kind of response which might well be expected of a second-generation panth passing through a predictable process of self-definition and crystallization.

One innovation attributed to Guru Amar Das can be regarded as strictly administrative. As the Panth expanded, new *saṅgat*s or congregations came into existence. Immediate contact with the Guru became increasingly difficult to maintain and it thus became necessary to appoint deputies authorized to act on his behalf. Guru Amar Das is traditionally credited with having established the *mañji* system of supervision, and the later *masand* system is believed to have developed from this prototype.[9]

Manji jurisdictions certainly existed at an early stage of the Panth's history, and, although their precise nature is exceedingly vague, there can be little doubt concerning the role and authority of the masands. These were men who supervised individual sangats or clusters of sangats on behalf of the Guru, probably acting as spiritual guides and certainly empowered to collect the tithes or other contributions which a loyal Sikh might be expected to give to his Master. The masand system lasted until its formal abolition by Guru Gobind Singh in 1699.

A second innovation which is usually attributed to the third Guru concerns the institutionalizing of a key doctrine. Guru Nanak had made it abundantly clear that caste status (like all exterior conventions) could have no bearing on access to the divine Name and thus to the means of liberation. It was probably Guru Amar Das who borrowed from the Sufis the practice of compulsory commensality, thereby giving practical expression to the first Guru's ideal. In the Sikh tradition this inter-dining convention emerged as the *laṅgar*. This convention requires men and women of all castes to sit in status-free lines (*paṅgat*) and eat together

---

[9] Ibid. 42. A *mañji*, literally a string-bed, designated authority over a sangat or group of sangats. *Masand*, derived from *masnad* or 'throne', came to be applied to the person who sat upon the manji. Traditionally the appointment to manjis is believed to date from the time of third Guru, and the masand system from the time of the fourth. Kahn Singh Nabha, *Guruśabad ratanākar mahān koś* (2nd rev. edn., Patiala, 1960), 750, 698. Fauja Singh argues persuasively that the manjis were actually preachers and they did not possess any territorial jurisdiction. *Guru Amar Das: Life and Teachings* (New Delhi, 1979), 116–29.

when they assemble on the sacred ground of the *dharam-sālā* or *gurduārā* (gurdwara).[10]

The langar is a particularly obscure institution as far as its period of introduction is concerned, but there can be no doubt concerning the central importance which it acquired nor the reason for actually introducing it. Caste is a contentious issue to which we must return. Here we note the early introduction of a convention which struck at a major aspect of caste, thereby advancing the process of defining a distinctive Sikh identity.

The third variety of innovation comprises a cluster of decisions (conscious or implicit) which concerned the developing ritual of the Panth. Whereas the langar plainly matched the intention of Guru Nanak, the new practices which together supply a distinctive panthic ritual might well seem to be in conflict with it. The first Guru had stressed the interior nature of devotion, dismissing as false and dangerous the kind of external ritual associated with conventional Hindu tradition or the orthodox Islam of the mullah. Decisions attributed to the third Guru may look suspiciously like the kind of thing which Nanak execrated. They include the digging of a sacred well (*bāolī*) in the Guru's village of Goindval to serve as a place of pilgrimage for Sikhs. They also include the introduction of particular festival days and the compiling of a collection which was later to become a sacred scripture.[11] Guru Amar Das is also credited with the decision to excavate the sacred pool which marked the founding of Amritsar.[12]

There are two answers which can be given to the problem thus presented. The theological answer is that the Guru is one and that decisions made by the third Guru proceed from precisely the same source as attitudes expressed by the first. This answer implies the second response, which is that changed circumstances require fresh decisions. No one is likely to be surprised by this development. A growing and maturing Panth could never have sustained the informality of the first Guru's practice. The formalizing of the tradition occurs at precisely the period when one would expect it and in much the manner that we might anticipate.

One last development deserves to be noted before we conclude this survey of the early Nanak-panth and turn to an examination of its actual

[10] McLeod, *Gurū Nānak and the Sikh Religion*, p. 210.

[11] McLeod, *The Evolution of the Sikh Community*, pp. 7–8.

[12] Kahn Singh, *Guruśabad ratanākar mahān koś*, p. 57. The actual excavation was conducted by Guru Ram Das. Ibid. McLeod (trans.), *Textual Sources for the Study of Sikhism*, pp. 28–9.

beliefs and practices. This is the critically important compiling of a sacred scripture by Guru Arjan in 1603–4. Guru Amar Das had evidently commissioned a preliminary compilation (the so-called Goindval *pothīs*) and the fifth Guru is believed to have used this prototype when producing the larger definitive version. The result was the Adi Granth.[13] There are unsolved textual problems associated with the Adi Granth, but none of these affect the powerfully cohesive role which the scripture was to assume during the later history of the Panth.

The death of Guru Arjan in 1606 marks a significant turning-point in the development of the Panth. Difficulties had emerged in the Panth's relationship with the local Mughal authorities and the hostility which fitfully developed during the course of the succeeding century has traditionally been held to account for the significant changes which eventually transformed the Panth. The analysis is rather more complex than this traditional summary might suggest and to that analysis we shall return in the next chapter. There can be no doubt, however, that the deteriorating relationship with Mughal authority supplies a large part of the explanation and that Guru Arjan's death in Mughal custody provides an appropriate symbol for the change which was taking place. Needless to say it is not a sudden change, instantly transforming the Nanak-panth of the sixteenth century into a prototype of the eighteenth-century Khalsa. The continuities remain evident and much that we may affirm concerning the early Panth applies with equal force to its seventeenth-century successor.

The permanence of the Nanak-panth was thus ensured by ritual and administrative measures introduced by the early Gurus. To what extent did the growing and crystallizing Panth present the authentic doctrines and ideals of the first Guru? There are two answers to be given to this question, the first of which has already been indicated. The early successors who followed Nanak as Guru continued to present the same teachings, cast in the same format and expressed in a very similar idiom. There is a developing richness in the poetry of the tradition, a trend which was significantly advanced during the period of Guru Arjan (1581–1606).[14] In terms of doctrinal content, however, the tradition remained essentially the same as that which Nanak had delivered to the first Sikhs.

---

[13] McLeod, *The Evolution of the Sikh Community*, pp. 60–1.

[14] Guru Arjan is the most prolific of all the contributors to the Adi Granth. Amongst his many compositions, his lengthy *Sukhmani* in *Gauṛi* raga stands out (Adi Granth, pp. 262–96).

This response obviously describes a fundamental aspect of the early Nanak-panth, one which should certainly not be neglected. If, however, we are to achieve a balanced perspective, it must be accompanied by the second of the required answers. The second answer distinguishes the leaders of the Panth from the bulk of its adherents. By consulting the Adi Granth or the works of Bhai Gurdas, we encounter a normative response, an interpretation of the divine Name message as understood by the guides and leaders of the Panth. The full measure of Nanak's teachings demands a portion of our attention because it continues to inform the understanding of the Panth's acknowledged leadership during the pre-Khalsa period. There is, however, another range of understanding and to this more popular concept of Gurmat we must now turn.

The principal source for the popular variety of understanding is supplied by the janam-sakhis. The janam-sakhis are traditional narratives of the life of Baba Nanak, collections of anecdotes which relate in fond detail a wealth of stories concerning the first Guru. As records of accurate history or biography they must normally be discarded, but in so doing we must avoid any suggestion that the janam-sakhis provide source material of limited value. Properly understood, the janam-sakhis are very valuable indeed, quite apart from the endless fascination which their many anecdotes can supply. The janam-sakhis are properly understood as hagiography; and their appropriate context is not the lifetime of the first Guru but the later period within which they actually developed. Trustworthy information concerning the life of Guru Nanak is not what they supply. What they do provide is useful testimony to the life and understanding of the early Panth.[15]

This should not imply that the janam-sakhis will always yield their information easily. There are two general problems which must confront any attempt to use them as sources for the life of the early Panth. The first derives from the fact that the earliest of the surviving janam-sakhis belongs to the mid-seventeenth century and that prior to the eighteenth century it stands alone.[16] Although there can be no doubt that oral growth dates from the sixteenth century, the actual evidence belongs to a later period. It thus requires a process of careful deduction if we are to utilize the janam-sakhis as sources for the life and beliefs of the early Panth.

The second problem also demands careful analysis. Because the

---

[15] For a study of the janam-sakhis, see W. H. McLeod, *Early Sikh Tradition: A Study of the Janam-sākhīs* (Oxford, 1980).

[16] Ibid. 13, 19.

narrators and compilers of the janam-sakhis had their attention consciously focused on an earlier period, the contemporary information which they deliver is implicit rather than direct, nested within the story cycles which they generated. This may enhance its claims to authenticity. It also presents us with problems of exegesis and interpretation.[17]

This certainly does not mean, however, that the janam-sakhi contribution is invariably an obscure one. On the contrary, it delivers a distinct impression of the popular image of Nanak and also of the manner in which many devout Sikhs evidently applied his teachings. The image which they present is indicated by their strong preference for the title 'Baba' rather than for 'Guru'. The latter title does appear, particularly when Nanak's role as the Great Teacher is brought into focus, but typically he is Baba Nanak. As such he represents piety and spiritual wisdom, the supreme exemplar of the only sure path to deliverance.[18] All who acknowledge him as Master and practise the simple discipline which he enjoined will find peace in this present world and liberation in the hereafter.

The discipline which Baba Nanak is believed to have taught is indeed a simple one and it is here that we find ourselves drawn dramatically away from his actual teachings and from the faithful replicas which his successors produced. The janam-sakhis project a much less subtle understanding of the key doctrine of the *nām* and of its practical expression in the discipline of *nām simaraṇ*. This is plainly evident from a standard formula incorporated in the conclusion to many individual anecdotes. A common variety of anecdote (*sākhī*) records how Baba Nanak visited a particular place during his travels, converted the people by means of a miracle or wise pronouncement, and then proceeded on his way. One such anecdote relates how he conferred grain and fire on a people who possessed neither. It concludes:

And so Baba Nanak gave them grain and fire. The entire population of that land became Sikhs. They took up repeating 'Guru, Guru' and in every house a dharamsala was established. Guru Baba Nanak taught them the three-fold discipline of repeating the divine Name, giving charity, and regular bathing [*nām dān iśnān*]. Everyone in that land declared, 'Blessed is our destiny that we have beheld your presence and that your feet have trodden in this land.'[19]

---

[17] Ibid. 248–67.   [18] Ibid. 250–2.

[19] W. H. McLeod (trans.), *The B40 Janam-sākhī* (Amritsar, 1980), 187. Brackets have been removed from this translation and the words *nām dān iśnān* have been indicated. Although the third word of the *nām dān iśnān* formula is now conceived as an injunction to live a pure life, the janam-sakhi understanding was plainly the literal sense of regular bathing. McLeod, *Early Sikh Tradition*, pp. 263–4.

From this and many other examples it is evident that *nām simaraṇ* was understood as a mechanical repetition of the single word 'Guru'. This, it may be argued, is a part of the total range covered by the concept of *nām simaraṇ*, but plainly it lacks the sophistication of Nanak's own understanding.

One other feature of this standard conclusion deserves to be noted. In every house, we are told, a dharamsala was established.[20] In other words, each house became a place where devout Sikhs would gather to sing the Gurus' hymns. The twin concepts of sangat and *kīrtan* or hymn-singing are thus emphasized in the janam-sakhis as a regular feature of the corporate life of the Nanak-panth. Elsewhere in the janam-sakhis we encounter a reference which indicates that the dharamsala was one of the features which conferred a distinctive identity on the Nanak-panth. Sikhs of Guru Nanak can be distinguished from adherents of other panths because they possess their own special place of worship. Vaishnavas have their temple, Yogis have their *āsaṇ*, Muslims have their mosque, and Nanak-panthis have their dharamsala.[21]

This same passage from the *B40 Janam-sākhī* also claims that Nanak-panthis are distinguished by a unique salutation (*pairī pavaṇā satigurū hoiā*) and by the customary *nām dān iśnān* ideal.[22] A comment of this kind should be treated with caution, and we should not read too much into a single reference from an eighteenth-century janam-sakhi. There are, however, other indications which strengthen the impression of an emergent panth, one which is still in the process of drawing its own boundaries and defining its own distinctive identity. One such indicator is the clear janam-sakhi recognition of Guru Angad as the chosen successor, a feature which offers firm proof of an established lineage. Another is the prominence which they give to Baba Nanak's disputations with representatives of other recognized panths.[23]

In contrast to these positive indications we must also note features which imply hesitation. Nanak's janam-sakhi contestants conspicuously include Hindu pandits, Muslim qazis, and Nath yogis (the latter including the great Guru Gorakhnath himself.[24] Were such encounters

[20] McLeod (trans.), *The B40 Janam-sākhī*, p. 206. Id., *Early Sikh Tradition*, p. 261. *Vārāṅ Bhāī Gurdās* 1: 27. The term *gurduārā* was later adopted as the name of the place where the Gurus' hymns were sung. W. H. McLeod, *The Sikhs* (New York, 1989), p. 57.

[21] McLeod (trans.), *The B40 Janam-sākhī*, p. 143. Id., *Early Sikh Tradition*, pp. 260–1.

[22] McLeod (trans), *The B40 Janam-sākhī*, pp. 142–3.

[23] The *Purātan Janam-sākhī* (5th edn. Amritsar, 1959) provides examples of the first feature on pp. 107–8, 110; and of the second on pp. 16–20, 22–4, 26–8, 40–5, 52–6, 66–70, 72, 80–1, 82–6, 96–106, and 108–10.

[24] A famous occasion occurs in the *Purātan* janam-sakhis, sakhi 54.

restricted to these three varieties of contestant, the sense of separateness would be very strong indeed. The effect is, however, diminished by implied comparisons with Vaishnavas, by the suggestion that Nanak might adopt various panthic identities,[25] and by the occasional claim that he regarded himself as a Hindu.[26]

These conflicting indicators point to a single definite conclusion. The Nanak-panth as refracted through the janam-sakhis can be recognized as a panth which is in the process of self-definition but which has not yet achieved a clear awareness of separate identity. This, it seems, was the status of the pre-Khalsa Nanak-panth and also of those adherents who retained a Nanak-panthi identity during the eighteenth century and beyond. It is, in other words, strictly an emergent panth. It is in the process of becoming without any certain awareness of having arrived.

This, we must stress, is a popular view of the Panth. References which can be cited from the works of both Guru Arjan and Bhai Gurdas offer some support for the claim that the leaders of the Nanak-panth had developed a strong sense of panthic identity by the end of the sixteenth century.[27] Such references match the reasonable expectation that the intellectual élite within the Panth moved more rapidly towards a sense of distinct identity than did the body of believers. Those who constituted the bulk of the Panth were much more exposed to inclusive ideals and blurred identities. There is nothing surprising about this. The same difference persists throughout the entire history of the Panth and, although it has receded during the last hundred years (particularly since 1947), there remains clear evidence of its presence today.[28]

This difference must be kept in mind whenever any attempt is made to define Gurmat or the distinctive Sikh identity. In the case of the early Nanak-panth the conclusion which follows is that no clear line of demarcation can be drawn in order to separate it from contiguous Hindu tradition. This does not mean, however, that the Nanak-panth lacked definition or the kind of distinctive ideals which signalled a conscious Nanak-panthi identity. In general terms this identity was defined by a

---

[25] McLeod (trans.), *The B40 Janam-sākhī*, p. 161.

[26] Ibid. 84, 148. Piar Singh (samp.), *Śambhū Nāth vālī janam patrī Bābe Nānak Jī kī prasidh nān Ādi Sākhīān* (Patiala, 1969), 24, 42.

[27] Guru Arjan, *Bhairau* 3, Adi Granth, p. 1136. *Vārān Bhāī Gurdās* 1: 21, 33: 2, 33: 4. Although the hymn attributed to Guru Arjan in Bhairau raga bears the signature of Kabir in the closing couplet and has a parallel in the *Kabīr-granthāvalī*, it is safe to assume that Guru Arjan would have accepted what it says: 'We are neither Hindu nor Musalaman'. The hymn is prefaced with his symbol and he after all compiled the Adi Granth.

[28] Paul Hershman, *Punjabi Kinship and Marriage* (Delhi, 1981), 24.

common loyalty, by common association, and by common practice.[29]
Any man or woman who acknowledged the loyalty and joined with
others to observe a particular pattern of worship would be plainly
identified as a Sikh of Guru Nanak. The boundaries might be indistinct,
but not the centre.

In specific terms the common loyalty was, of course, veneration for
Nanak and for the legitimate succession of Gurus who followed him in
the lineage which he had established. The stress is powerfully on the first
of the Gurus, a feature which is indicated by the janam-sakhi focus on
Nanak and through the conventional use of his name by the successors
whose works appear in the Adi Granth.[30] The nature of the loyalty
undergoes a progressive change as the Baba image of Nanak is displaced
by the Guru image, and as the Guru status is supplemented by the
attributes of royalty. The lineage which commences with the humble
Sant ideal is thereby transformed into a succession of 'True Kings' (*sachā
pādaśāh*). None of this, however, affects the basic assumption that all
who regard themselves as Sikhs will acknowledge fealty to this spiritual
lineage.

The custom of gathering as a *satsaṅg* for regular kirtan sessions was
also a specific and essential feature of the Nanak-panthi identity.[31] The
convention derived from the traditional Sant emphasis on the value of
associating with the truly devout, an experience which enabled the
humble participant to acquire a portion of the merit which emanated
from the true *sādh*. It was greatly strengthened by the practice of singing
the Gurus' own compositions at such gatherings and it was this latter
feature which gave the Nanak-panthi gathering its own distinctive
identity.

The singing of kirtan in the context of the satsang was not a ritual
unique to the Nanak-panth. It was rather the nature of the kirtan which
imparted distinction. The practice encouraged a particular concept of the
śabad or divine Word, and, together with the actual recording of the
Gurus' compositions as a scripture, it prepared the way for a fundamental doctrine. The doctrine which it foreshadowed affirms the eternal
presence of the mystical Guru within the sacred scripture and wherever
his followers gather as an assembly of the Panth.

---

[29] *Vārān Bhāi Gurdās* 28: 15.
[30] The Adi Granth uses the term *mahalā* to identify the works of the various Gurus
(*mahalā 1* designating Guru Nanak, *mahalā 2* Guru Angad, etc.). All five of the Gurus who
follow Guru Nanak, however, employ the name Nanak as a signature in the final couplet.
[31] *Vārān Bhāi Gurdās* 40: 11.

True to the teachings of the Gurus, these assemblies were obviously intended to be open to men and women of all castes. As we have already noted, this seems plainly to have been the essential purpose of requiring all who attended a ritual gathering of Sikhs to eat together in the langar. Although its primary purpose may well have been evaded by many Sikhs, it continued to be honoured as a Nanak-panthi ideal. This is not to suggest that the early Panth was casteless. What it does indicate is a continuing loyalty to the first Guru's insistence that caste had nothing to do with access to liberation.

Caste was, in fact, present and acknowledged within the Nanak-panth. The eleventh *vār* of Bhai Gurdas lists the names of prominent followers of the early Gurus,[32] thus enabling us to reconstruct a general profile of the Panth's leadership during the sixteenth and early seventeenth centuries. In his list Bhai Gurdas commonly identifies individual caste identities, and in so doing he indicates that one caste was particularly prominent in terms of leadership within the Panth. This was the Khatri caste, the caste to which all the Gurus belonged. The janam-sakhis support this feature and supply names which enable us to identify the other castes which were also conspicuously represented within the Panth. After the Khatris the principal contributors to janam-sakhi anecdotes are Jats, and they in turn are followed by members of artisan castes (notably Tarkhans or carpenters).[33]

None of this comes as any surprise. The janam-sakhis are strongly rural in tone and all three castes are to be found in rural Punjab.[34] When eventually the British began to enumerate Punjabi society, these three caste groups all emerged as prominent constituents of the Panth. The notable addition is the outcaste or untouchable Sikhs. The conspicuous attachment of the Mirasi minstrel Mardana to Baba Nanak implies access for the lowly, but Mardana was not strictly an outcaste and, even as a follower of marginal status, he remains an exception. Others can be noted in the early evidence,[35] but it seems likely that a significant outcaste membership did not develop until a later period of the Panth's history.

Actual numbers and proportions are impossible to determine. Bhai Gurdas deals only with the more notable members of the Panth and, in view of the Khatri status in rural Punjab, their prominence in this regard

[32] Ibid. 11: 13–31.
[33] McLeod, *Early Sikh Tradition*, pp. 258–60.
[34] Ibid. 257–8.
[35] For example, there is Paira Chandali noted by Bhai Gurdas. *Vārān Bhāī Gurdās* 11: 24. Outcastes were certainly not excluded from the Sikh Panth.

is entirely predictable. The janam-sakhis, with their broader coverage, offer no obvious clues concerning the numerical strengths of the three discernible groups. British figures reveal a substantial Jat majority in the late nineteenth century[36] and it is possible that this numerical preponderance extends back to the Panth's earliest days. Here, however, we must acknowledge uncertainty. What is clear is that three caste groups are conspicuously present within the Panth and that no effort seems to have been made to conceal their identities.

This acknowledgement of caste identities was presumably acceptable to the Gurus, for it receives unselfconscious treatment from the impeccably orthodox Bhai Gurdas, and the Gurus themselves married their own children according to traditional caste prescriptions. The anti-caste thrust of the Gurus' teachings must thus be seen as a doctrine which referred to spiritual deliverance and to the assemblies which helped individuals to achieve that objective. It is also legitimate to deduce a firm rejection of injustice or hurtful discrimination based on caste status. What is not implied is a total obliteration of caste identity.[37]

In this and other respects the Nanak-panth seems to have been generally loyal to the intention and example of the Gurus. Their stress on interiority was evidently understood, and, although the practice of *nām simaraṇ* may have been greatly simplified, the Panth kept some appropriate targets in view. This, at least, is the clear message communicated by the persistent janam-sakhi attacks on the punctilious pandit, the bigoted qazi, and the ascetic yogi. These assaults also implied what elsewhere the janam-sakhis make perfectly plain, namely the obligation to live as ordinary men and women. Deliverance from the cycle of transmigration was to be achieved by remaining in the world, not by withdrawing into ritual or ascetic seclusion.

This, it seems, was the Nanak-panth which developed during the course of the sixteenth century, and it retained its characteristic features throughout the century which was to follow. Veneration for Nanak and his line of successors qualified a person as a Nanak-panthi or Sikh. To express this allegiance each Nanak-panthi gathered with others in sangats, there to sing the kirtan composed by their Gurus. Most sangats

[36] *Census of India 1881*, vol. 1, book 1 (Lahore, 1883), 107–8.

[37] When this point was made in *The Evolution of the Sikh Community*, it prompted the accusation that the Gurus were being labelled as insincere in their opposition to caste. This was not the case. The Gurus accepted the marital obligations of caste, but were totally opposed to the idea that caste involved any discrimination or that it had any bearing upon the individual's access to liberation. The latter, all-important to the Gurus, was provided by loyalty to the divine Name.

were under masands appointed by the Guru and to them Nanak-panthis made their offerings for transmitting to the Guru. Nanak-panthis recognized *nām simaraṇ* as a standard practice of the Panth, but for most of its members it was evidently understood as the repetition of a simple formula. A small group within the Panth, however, practised it as it had been taught by Guru Nanak and in the way it still continued to be taught by his successors.

Caste had no place within the sangat, at least amongst those that were loyal to the Gurus. Sikhs were free to observe it as a marriage convention, but it had no bearing on liberation from transmigration nor did it justify discrimination of any sort. As such it was not to be recognized in the gurdwaras and the langar was instituted to prevent it being so. Although certain days were set aside as particularly appropriate for visiting the Guru and paying him respects, the Nanak-panthi was not to withdraw from the responsibilities of the world. Liberation was to be found by singing kirtan and practising *nām simaraṇ* in the context of an ordinary life.

This pattern of Nanak-panthi devotion was practised throughout the sixteenth and seventeenth centuries. It was during the seventeenth century, however, that external influences began to impinge significantly, and eventually these influences led to a radical reshaping of the Panth. The sixth Guru signals the formal beginning of the process and the tenth Guru is traditionally believed to have carried it to a dramatic climax. As always the actual experience turns out to be more diverse and complex than the tradition would allow. It is an experience which we shall examine in the next chapter.

3

The Khalsa and its Rahit

To BE a Sikh at the beginning of the seventeenth century meant adherence to the Nanak-panth. This involved a professed veneration for Guru Nanak, continuing obedience to his legitimate successors, and regular association with others who acknowledged the same loyalty. Those who shared the same Nanak-panthi allegiance constituted local groups or sangats which gathered regularly in satsangs to sing the Gurus' hymns. Such gatherings took place in dharamsalas. Amongst the devout no caste barriers obstructed membership of the Panth or participation in its developing rituals, although caste identities were still recognized by Sikhs within the larger Punjabi society to which they belonged. A substantial majority of Sikhs were rural folk, most of them belonging to trader, cultivator, or artisan castes.

Special festival days had been appointed for observance by the Panth and on such occasions Sikhs would reverently visit the Guru or gather at places which had acquired pious associations. One location was regarded with particular respect by the end of the sixteenth century. This was Ramdaspur or Amritsar, and it was there that the fifth Guru supervised the compiling of a sacred scripture for the Panth. The Guru remained the key figure within the Nanak-panth, the object of devout veneration and source of continuing guidance.

Early in the seventeenth century that guidance seemed to be undergoing a significant change. Hargobind had succeeded his father Arjan as Guru in 1606 and the ever-faithful Bhai Gurdas reflects the concern which soon developed within the Panth. In a famous stanza from his *Vār* 26 he gives expression to criticisms which the sixth Guru evidently attracted.

> The earlier Gurus sat peacefully in dharamsalas; this one roams the land.
> Emperors visited their homes with reverence; this one they cast into jail.
> No rest for his followers, ever active; their restless Master has fear of none.
> The earlier Gurus sat graciously blessing; this one goes hunting with dogs.

> They had servants who harboured no malice; this one encourages
> scoundrels.

These are the criticisms. They are immediately followed by an assertion
of the author's own continuing loyalty.

> Yet none of these changes conceals the truth; the Sikhs are still drawn as
> bees to the lotus.
> The truth stands firm, eternal, changeless; and pride still lies subdued.[1]

Guru Hargobind had adopted a new policy, one which tradition
dramatically expresses in the donning of two symbolic swords. One
sword represented the continuing spiritual authority (*pīrī*) which he had
inherited from his five predecessors. The other proclaimed a newly
assumed temporal power (*mīrī*). The Panth was to become more than an
assembly of the devout, and its Guru was thereafter to wield an authority
more expansive than that of his predecessors.[2]

A new building is also believed to have symbolized the same change.
No one can be sure precisely when Akal Takhat was first erected, but
Sikh tradition insistently maintains that it first appeared during the time
of Guru Hargobind and that it has ever since represented the same ideal
as the doctrine of *mīrī–pīrī*.[3] Akal Takhat faces Harimandir (the Golden
Temple), and, whereas Harimandir symbolizes the spiritual message of
the Gurus, it is Akal Takhat which represents their temporal authority.
Together with the appearance of weapons, horses, dogs, and hunting
expeditions, Akal Takhat also serves to represent the growing militancy
of the Panth. The dual concept, whatever its actual origin, is traditionally
located in the period and in the intention of Guru Hargobind. In its
developed form it was to reflect a transformed Panth.

The actual reason for this significant shift in the nature and policy of

---

[1] *Vārān Bhāī Gurdās* 26: 24.

[2] Kahn Singh Nabha, *Guruśabad ratanākar mahān koś* (2nd rev. edn., Patiala, 1960),
198.

[3] The traditional date is s. 1665 (AD 1608–9). (s is the abbreviation for Samvat, used for
dating according to the Vikrami era which begins approximately $56\frac{3}{4}$ years before the
Christian era.) Ibid. 27, 198. The modern Akal Takhat was destroyed by the Indian Army in
its attack on the Golden Temple complex in June 1984, and Jarnail Singh Bhindranwale
was killed while defending it. It was immediately rebuilt, ostensibly by a Nihang chieftain
Santa Singh but in fact by covert government assistance. Sikhs opposed to the central
government immediately tore down the new building and are now engaged in erecting a
much bigger one. For accounts of Akal Takhat prior to 1984, see Bhagat Singh in Fauja
Singh (ed.), *The City of Amritsar: A Study of Historical, Cultural, Social and Economic
Aspects* (New Delhi, 1978), 42–58; and Madanjit Kaur, *The Golden Temple Past and
Present* (Amritsar, 1983), 168–72. A popular account is Harjinder Singh Dilgeer, *The Akal
Takhat* (Jullundur, 1980), reissued as *Glory of the Akal Takhat* (Jullundur, 1984).

the Panth remains a subject of debate. Tradition delivers one answer and there can be no doubt that the traditional answer is at least partly correct. The sixth Guru, witnessing the increasing tyranny of the Mughal rulers, assumed an enlarged authority and armed his followers in order to resist their evil deeds. A modified version of the tradition views it as an essentially defensive move. Both variants offer Mughal threats as the reason and both interpret the change as a deliberate decision by the Guru to arm a Panth which had hitherto been peaceable and weaponless.

There is no evident reason why this response theory should be denied. There is, however, good reason for introducing a supplementary cause and it is this additional element which has generated some controversy in recent years. The supplementary claim focuses on the undeniable presence of Jats in the early Panth and it suggests that in becoming Sikhs they will have remained Jats. In other words, they are most unlikely to have shed the militant traditions which they certainly inherited as a major feature of their Jat culture.[4]

It accordingly seems necessary to assume that militant traditions were already present within the Panth by the time Hargobind became Guru in 1606. If this is correct, it means that the standard explanation can be accepted only in the sense that a decision by Guru Hargobind represented a formal adoption of militant means and a corresponding change in the Guru's own life style. In an informal sense militant traditions were already well represented within the Panth and the Guru's change of policy served to harness these traditions to a developing need rather than introduce them for the first time. Contemporary circumstances thus encouraged a process whereby the traditions of a significant segment within the Panth increasingly became the acknowledged policy of the Panth as a whole. To this extent the traditional explanation seems eminently plausible. Alone it remains inadequate.

During the middle decades of the seventeenth century the threat receded and during this period the Panth continued to live a life resembling that of its early experience. Serious trouble returned during the later years of Guru Tegh Bahadur (1664–75). This involved renewed and increasingly serious hostility on the part of the Mughals, a condition which Sikh tradition attributes directly to the bigoted policy of the

---

[4] The significance of Jats and Jat culture on the developing Panth was raised in W. H. McLeod, *The Evolution of the Sikh Community* (Oxford, 1976), chaps. 1 and 3. Amongst the responses produced by this tentative enquiry the most notable was perhaps Jagjit Singh, *Perspectives on Sikh Studies* (New Delhi, 1985), section 2. This section was reprinted (with amendments designed to make the criticisms more specific) in Gurdev Singh (ed.), *Perspectives on the Sikh Tradition* (Patiala, 1986), 326–85.

Emperor Aurangzeb. According to the dominant tradition, Guru Tegh Bahadur decided to confront Mughal power in response to a plea from Kashmiri Brahmans threatened with forcible conversion to Islam. He allowed himself to be arrested and executed in order that Mughal tyranny might stand revealed and that brave men might rise against it.[5]

Three themes are implicit in this tradition. The first is that Mughal rule spelt oppression and injustice. Though initially restricted to the Mughals, this theme was later to involve hostility towards Muslims as such. The second theme is the need to protect time-honoured conventions, notably those associated with Hindu tradition. The third, which is denied by the Guru's action but which follows as a deduction, is the ultimate need for force as a means of combating extreme injustice.

The tradition thus legitimizes the developments which were soon to follow. The protection theme is modified in that the rampart becomes *dharma* rather than Hindu rights; and *dharma* is variously conceived as the pattern of belief embodied in the Panth or as the moral order generally. With this amendment the three themes together supply the traditional interpretation of the crucial century which lies ahead. The moral order has been assaulted by evil men and, because the attack is fierce, those who would defend *dharma* must do so by means of the sword.[6] The assailants are Muslims, first Mughals and then Afghans. The defenders are to be Sikhs of a very special kind.

Here (as always) we are involved in the counterpoint of history and tradition, in the reciprocal interchange between the actual course of events in all its complexity and the comparatively simple interpretations with which those events are glossed. This is not to suggest that we should dismiss the latter and concentrate our attention only on the former. For present purposes that would be altogether inappropriate. If we are seeking answers to the question 'What is Sikhism?' or 'Who is a Sikh?', the double focus must be maintained. Traditional interpretations can be just as important as the actual facts and typically they are the more important. This is an axiom which needs to be kept clearly in mind as we venture upon the founding of the Khalsa and its development during the eighteenth century.

Tradition offers three inter-connected reasons for the founding of the Khalsa. The first derives directly from the scene of Guru Tegh Bahadur's execution, where, it is maintained, the Sikhs who were present shrank

[5] Harbans Singh, *Guru Tegh Bahadur* (New Delhi, 1982), 94–6. Trilochan Singh, *Guru Tegh Bahadur: Prophet and Martyr* (Delhi, 1967), 293–300.

[6] *Zafar-nāmā* 22, Dasam Granth, p. 1390.

from recognition for fear that they might suffer a like fate. Guru Gobind Singh, having learnt of their cowardice, determined to impose on his followers an outward form which would make them instantly recognizable. This would ensure that never again would Sikhs be able to take refuge in anonymity.[7]

The second of the traditional reasons focuses on the general problem of tyranny and injustice rather than on the specific instance provided by the ninth Guru's execution. According to this variant tradition, Guru Gobind Singh had realized that his Sikhs were mere sparrows, weak and timorous creatures who could never be trusted to face armed injustice without taking instant flight. The problem could be traced to the docile beliefs and customs which they had inherited, to traditions which might be appropriate in times of peace and order but which could never withstand the assaults of violent tyranny. Steel was needed, steel in their hands and steel in the soul of the Panth. Ratan Singh Bhangu, raised during the heroic years of the eighteenth century, gives forthright expression to this view in his *Prāchīn Panth Prakāś*. He concludes:

Thus the Guru reasoned and from thought he proceeded to action. His followers were to emerge as splendid warriors, their uncut hair bound in turbans; and as warriors all were to bear the name 'Singh' [lion]. This, the Guru knew, would be effective. He devised a form of baptism administered with the sword, one which would create a Khalsa staunch and unyielding. His followers would destroy the empire, each Sikh horseman believing himself to be a king. All weakness would be beaten out of them and each, having taken the baptism of the sword, would thereafter be firmly attached to the sword.[8]

The third reason concerns the internal administration of the Panth. As we noted earlier, the problem of increasing numbers and geographical dispersion had been met first by developing the manji system and then by delegating authority to deputies called masands.[9] A century later many of the masands had acquired corrupt ways and an overweening arrogance. The Guru accordingly decided to disestablish the masands and summon all Sikhs to place themeselves under his own direct supervision. As such they would become members of his k͟hālis or k͟hālsā, that portion of the royal domain which remained under the direct supervision of the central authority.[10]

---

[7] W. H. McLeod (trans.), *The Chaupā Siṅgh Rahit-nāmā* (Dunedin, 1987), section 166, p. 168.

[8] Ratan Singh Bhangu, *Prāchīn Panth Prakāś* 16: 32–6. Vir Singh edn. (Amritsar, 1962), 42.   [9] See chap. 2, n. 9.

[10] Ganda Singh (samp.), *Kavī Saināpati rachit Srī Gur Sobhā* (Patiala, 1967), 5: 6, 5: 25, 5: 30, pp. 20, 23–4 (Gurmukhi pagination).

Although there is nothing intrinsically implausible in any of these reasons, or in a selective combination of all three, we must nevertheless maintain our insistent distinction between history and tradition. We are here dealing with tradition, with *post facto* interpretations which express a later understanding and which recast earlier events in the light of subsequent developments. The distinction between history and tradition must be maintained notwithstanding the fact that one feature of the composite explanation can be strongly argued on the basis of etymology and other objective evidence. This concerns the role of the masands as a possible reason for the founding of the Khalsa as a formal order.[11] With the possible exception of this item we must deal with obscure history on the one hand and clear if variant tradition on the other.

The contrast becomes even more marked when we move from the reasons for the event to the actual event itself. From the traditional narratives we receive singularly dramatic accounts of what took place on Baisakhi Day 1699. The Guru is said to have circulated instructions that the regular Baisakhi Day assembly should be regarded as a particularly important one on this occasion. In response to the message a vast concourse gathered at Anandpur, eagerly awaiting the appearance of the Guru. When he stood before them he shocked all present into stunned silence by demanding the heads of five loyal Sikhs. His insistent demand finally produced a volunteer who was led into a nearby tent. A thud was heard and the Guru, emerging with a blood-stained sword, called for a second head. Eventually he secured five volunteers, each of them taken into the tent and there apparently dispatched.

The Guru then drew back the side of the tent, dramatically revealing five living Sikhs and five decapitated goats. The Sikhs were the *pañj piāre*, the 'cherished five' who had so convincingly demonstrated their total trust and loyalty. There were then initiated as the first members of the Khalsa order, and having completed the ceremony Guru Gobind Singh himself received initiation from their hands. For the ceremony he had provided an iron pot containing water into which one of his wives cast soluble sweets. The sweetened water, stirred with a two-edged sword, was the *amrit* with which each entrant was initiated. Some of the *amrit* was applied to the face and hair, and some was drunk. All were thus required to drink from the same vessel regardless of caste and subsequently all were given *kaṛāh prasād* from a single iron pan. The rejection of caste distinctions, inherited from Nanak and transmitted by

[11] J. S. Grewal, *From Guru Nanak to Maharaja Ranjit Singh: Essays in Sikh History* (Amritsar, 1972), 60–1.

his successors, was thus given ritual expression in the *pāhul* or initiation ceremony of the Khalsa.[12]

Properly told in all its vivid detail, the story is an unusually dramatic one, and it will seem churlish to suggest that it cannot be entirely true. If we are writing one sort of history, the obligation to do so is inescapable and the task has been very effectively discharged in a masterly essay by Professor J. S. Grewal of Amritsar. Professor Grewal does not deny that an important event took place at Anandpur Sahib on Baisakhi Day 1699, nor does he reject all the details traditionally associated with the occasion. He does, however, criticize the manner in which the available source materials have been used by other historians. Having shown that some features must certainly be discarded, he concludes that judgement should be suspended on many other points pending careful research which has yet to be done.[13]

Another sort of history (and a perfectly legitimate one) frees us from this obligation. If we are seeking to understand the fashioning of a Sikh identity, we can remain uncommitted as far as most of the details are concerned. It matters little whether five volunteers were actually summoned or whether five goats were actually slain. The overriding fact is that in its essential outline the story is firmly believed and that this belief has unquestionably contributed to the subsequent shaping of conventional Sikh attitudes.

Having thus evaded a significant portion of the historian's usual responsibility, we must acknowledge that our quest for Sikh identity requires us to examine one particular feature of the Anandpur event in some detail. According to the traditional narratives, Guru Gobind Singh included in the inaugural ceremony a sermon, and in this sermon he is said to have enunciated the way of life which each initiant was thereafter to follow. The injunctions supplied in this sermon supplemented certain key items incorporated in the actual *pāhul* ceremony. Together they constitute the substance of the Rahit, the only significant additions being those which the Guru delivered immediately prior to his death in 1708.[14] Such at least is the traditional view, and, because the Rahit is so

---

[12] Gian Singh, *Tavārīkh Gurū Khālsā* (2nd edn., Patiala, 1970), 856–61. M. A. Macauliffe, *The Sikh Religion: Its Gurus, Sacred Writings and Authors* (Oxford, 1909), v. 91–7. The lengthy *Tavārīkh Gurū Khālsā* was published between 1891 and 1919.

[13] J. S. Grewal, 'The Khalsa of Guru Gobind Singh' in *From Guru Nanak to Maharaja Ranjit Singh*, chap. ix.

[14] Macauliffe, *The Sikh Religion*, v. 93–7, 243–5. Khushwant Singh, *A History of the Sikhs*, i (Princeton, 1963), 83–6, 95.

intimately related to the question of identity, it is an aspect of the traditional account which plainly we cannot avoid.

'Rahit' is one of those words which, because it expresses a fundamental concept, deserves to be much better known.[15] Indeed, it deserves (like 'Panth') to be a part of standard English usage, at least for anyone interested in the Sikhs and their tradition. Kahn Singh defines the word as follows: 'The systematic statement of Sikh principles; the way of life lived in accordance with the principles of the Sikh religion.'[16] This is an interestingly inaccurate definition. It is significant because it draws us back to the problem which so persistently frustrates all attempts to produce a simple comprehensive statement of Sikh identity. Kahn Singh was committed to the view that authentic Sikhism was represented by the Khalsa mode and he accordingly uses the terms 'Sikh' and 'Sikh religion' where correct usage requires 'Khalsa' and 'Khalsa tradition'. If, however, we make these substitutions, his brief definition can be accepted. It is the way of life enunciated by the Khalsa tradition which is summarized in the word 'Rahit', and non-Khalsa Sikhs sustain a separate identity precisely because they decline to observe some key features of the standard Rahit.

The Rahit is thus the Khalsa way of life, the system of belief and distinctive behaviour which all who accept Khalsa initiation are expected to observe. Since the eighteenth century various attempts have been made to express the Rahit in written form and the manuals thus produced are called rahit-namas.[17] Some of these manuals are very brief, concentrating on particular features of the Rahit as understood by their authors at the time of writing. The comprehensive rahit-nama en-

---

[15] The word derives from *rahaṇā*, 'to live'. The word is sometimes spelt 'Rahat' or 'Rehat'. The former transcribes a variant Punjabi version. The latter is incorrect.

[16] Kahn Singh, *Guruśabad ratanākar mahān koś*, p. 760.

[17] There are nine such works which date from before the middle of the nineteenth century. For the early rahit-namas, see below, pp. 36–9. Two extended prose rahit-namas which probably belong to the first half of the nineteenth century are *Prem Sumārg* and *Sau Sākhīān*. One which is available only in Punjabi is Randhir Singh (samp.), *Prem Sumārg Granth* (1953; 2nd edn., Jalandhar, 1965). The second one was issued in an English translation by Attar Singh of Bhadaur as *The Sakhee Book, or the Description of Gooroo Gobind Singh's Religion and Doctrines* (Banares, 1873). This was the version used by the Namdhari or Kuka Sikhs. See chap. 5, n. 6. A version has more recently been published in Punjabi by Gurbachan Singh Naiar (samp.), *Gur ratan māl arathāt sau sākhī* (Patiala, 1985). Since the founding of the Singh Sabha in 1873 the quest for an agreed rahit-nama has raised recurrent difficulty. Finally an acceptable version was published in 1950 under the title *Sikh Rahit Maryādā* and has sustained its position ever since. Most of *Sikh Rahit Maryādā* is in W. H. McLeod (trans.), *Textual Sources for the Study of Sikhism* (Manchester, 1984), 79–86. For further information see the introduction to McLeod (trans.), *The Chaupā Siṅgh Rahit-nāmā*; and id., 'The Problem of the Panjabi *rahit-nāmās*' in S. N. Mukherjee (ed.), *India: History and Thought* (Calcutta, 1982), 103–26.

deavours to cover all aspects of the Rahit and may venture into such areas as denunciation of the faithless or promises of a glory yet to come. In a comprehensive rahit-nama we can expect to find four recognizable elements, distinct in themselves yet closely related as aspects of the total Khalsa tradition.

The first element consists of the fundamental doctrines which an orthodox Sikh of the Khalsa is expected to affirm. These include such basic items as belief in Akal Purakh, veneration for the personal Gurus, and recognition of the mystical presence of the eternal Guru in the pages of the Adi Granth (the Guru Granth Sahib). This is normally the least conspicuous part of a rahit-nama. Such doctrines are obviously crucial features of the Khalsa faith and identity, and all that follows must necessarily be perceived as strictly compatible with these basic beliefs. As far as the rahit-namas are concerned, however, they can be largely taken for granted. For the purposes of enunciating the Rahit, a summary statement is usually accepted as adequate.

In passing we should note that this portion of a rahit-nama will typically incorporate much that the non-Khalsa Sikh can accept. Both Khalsa and non-Khalsa can affirm a certain range of common doctrine, a range which essentially corresponds to the earlier Nanak-panthi foundation. It is when we come to the three remaining components of a comprehensive rahit-nama that the critical differences emerge. These portions modify and extend the range of doctrine, building upon it an impressively detailed structure of personal behaviour and panthic ritual.

Rules for personal behaviour constitute the second component of a rahit-nama. These rules (which may be very detailed and specific) include instructions concerning the devotional obligations of a Khalsa Sikh, the outward forms by which Sikh men and women proclaim their identity, a variety of practices which are proscribed, and a list of particular groups with which a Khalsa should not associate. In a more developed rahit-nama the detail can be very considerable indeed, with injunctions covering a wide range of behaviour from personal devotion to elementary hygiene. Predictably there is a strong emphasis on features which express the militant aspect of the Khalsa identity, features which so obviously reflect the social constituency of the Panth and the experience of warfare which it encountered during the eighteenth century.

Some of the typical rahit-nama prescriptions derive from earlier Nanak-panthi practice and are thus congenial to all who claim to be Sikhs. They include an insistent emphasis on the personal performance of a specific daily liturgy (the *nit-nem*) and regular attendance at a gurdwara, there to pay one's respects and participate in corporate kirtan with other members of the gathered sangat. Other items define the distinctively Khalsa identity. All rahit-namas, regardless of their age or provenance, stress the paramount obligation of retaining the hair uncut, and as the tradition works its way through early uncertainties this provision eventually becomes one of the celebrated *pañj kakke* or Five Ks. These are five items of external appearance which all Khalsa Sikhs must wear, each beginning with the letter 'k'. In addition to the uncut hair (*kes*), the cluster comprises a wooden comb worn in the hair (*kaṅghā*), a steel bangle (*kaṛā*), a sword or dagger (*kirpān*), and a pair of breeches which must not reach below the knee (*kachh*).[18]

Conspicuous amongst the practices to be avoided is smoking tobacco, an injunction which was originally aimed at the hookah but which now includes the European pipe and cigarette.[19] The origin of this particular ban is not altogether clear. A possible reason could be the fact that a hookah would encumber a soldier and that the prohibition should accordingly be understood as one of the many military injunctions incorporated in the Rahit. Alternatively, the hookah may perhaps have been identified as a distinctively Muslim artefact. If this latter theory is correct, the item becomes one of the numerous anti-Muslim injunctions of the Rahit.

Muslims and their distinctive practices provide an explicit target for the early rahit-namas and some other surviving injunctions can be traced to this particular source. The most obvious is the ban on *halāl* meat. For the Khalsa, meat is permitted, provided that it is not beef and provided also that it comes from an animal killed with a single blow (*jhaṭkā*). This eliminates the possibility that it may have been polluted by Muslim ritual, for animals slain by the *halāl* process must bleed to death.[20]

In the modern rahit-namas this eighteenth-century attitude towards Muslims has been greatly softened, but a few remnants of its earlier prominence still survive. *Jhaṭkā* meat provides a rare example of one which still proclaims its origin. Usually the origin is concealed by a recasting produced in response to later circumstances. An early prohibition of sexual contact with Muslim women thus becomes a commandment directed against adultery in general.[21] It seems probable

[18] McLeod (trans.), *The Chaupā Siṅgh Rahit-nāmā*, pp. 32–44. *Sikh Rahit Maryādā* (Amritsar, 1983), 26.

[19] McLeod (trans.), *The Chaupā Siṅgh Rahit-nāmā*, sections 7a, 80, and 438, pp. 150, 156, and 182. *Sikh Rahit Maryādā*, p. 26.

[20] McLeod (trans.), *The Chaupā Siṅgh Rahit-nāmā*, section 372, p. 179.

[21] *Sikh Rahit Maryādā*, p. 26.

that, in like manner, an original ban on the Muslim hookah was sub-sequently converted into a rejection of tobacco smoking in general.

Most of the injunctions directed against other eighteenth-century rivals of the true Khalsa survive in the modern Rahit as interesting relics rather than as reconstituted components of essential behaviour. Who now cares about the minor panths listed as *pañj mel* or 'the five reprobate groups'?[22] In many other respects, however, the early tradition holds firm. The ban on both hair-cutting and smoking is certainly firm as far as orthodox opinion is concerned. These are two of the four gross sins which earn the title of *patit* or 'renegade' and which today require re-initiation if repentance is offered and accepted.[23]

The third element in a standard rahit-nama consists of orders for the conduct of Khalsa ceremonies. Once again the distinction between Khalsa and non-Khalsa Sikh emerges. Some of these rituals can, it is true, be practised by the latter as well as by the former. The tone and content of the modern orders is, however, strongly Khalsa and the principal rite is unambiguous in intention. The prime ritual of initiation is exclusively Khalsa, for thus does one accept its discipline and adopt its outward identity. In the standard modern version of the Rahit many of the personal injunctions are actually incorporated within this particular rite, recited as portions of a standard homily which must be delivered to all who take *pāhul*.[24]

The fourth element in a comprehensive rahit-nama presents the sanctions which are to be invoked in the case of offences against the Rahit. Procedures designed to enforce the Rahit have, in practice, been very difficult to define and even more difficult to apply consistently. This, at least, appears to be the modern experience and there is evidence which suggests that earlier generations suffered a similar problem.

Any Khalsa Sikh adjudged guilty of violating the Rahit is branded *tanakhāhīā* and the penance imposed on the offender is called a *tanakhāh*.[25] Both terms emerged during the eighteenth century, clearly

---

[22] There is agreement concerning three of the five reprobate groups. These are the Minas and Dhir-malias (the followers of relatives of the orthodox line who asserted claims to the title of Guru) and the Masands. The fourth and fifth are disputed. According to *Gur Sobhā* they were *naṛī-mār* (users of the hookah) and *kuṛī-mār* (killers of female daughters). In the *Chaupā Siṅgh Rahit-nāmā* it is the Ram-raias (the followers of a third schismatic claimant to the title of Guru) and the Masandias (those who follow the Masands). Kahn Singh identified the fifth as the Sir-gum, or those who cut their hair (*Guruśabad ratanākar mahān koś*, pp. 593–4). *Sikh Rahit Maryādā*, p. 27, generalizes it to cover 'other enemies of the Panth'.

[23] Ibid. 27–8.   [24] Ibid. 25–8.

[25] McLeod (trans.), *The Chaupā Siṅgh Rahit-nāmā*, pp. 25, 234 (n. 300).

demonstrating that effective enforcement of the Rahit has long been a major concern within the Khalsa. There are, however, few indications of precisely how enforcement procedures were applied during the eighteenth century. In recent times the process has necessarily been selective, concentrating on important individuals or on issues which happen to be conspicuously present in the public eye. Individual sangats certainly possess the authority to impose penances. This authority is delegated to five chosen representatives (*pañj piāre*) and a guilty verdict requires the performance of a penance if the offender is to remain an accepted member of the sangat.[26] In practice, however, this simple procedure is too often frustrated by indifference or circumvented by the internal dynamics of a sangat. It is one aspect of the problem of authority, a general problem to which we must return.

In thus defining and briefly describing the Rahit we have necessarily used expressions which indicate that the system is not a static one, that it has in fact continued to evolve during the three centuries which have elapsed since first it was formally promulgated. In theory this pattern of change and development need pose no problem. Although the line of personal Gurus ended with Guru Gobind Singh in 1708, the mystical Guru continues to dwell in the Granth and in the Panth, ever-available for the kind of situational guidance which changing circumstances require. It is, therefore, perfectly consistent for an authorized assembly of the Khalsa to speak as the Guru, provided only that its message does not conflict with anything contained in the Guru Granth Sahib. Given this doctrine of the continuing authority of the eternal Guru, there should be no problem as far as changes to the Rahit are concerned.

In practice, however, the issue is much more complex. This is partly because it can be exceedingly difficult to secure the kind of corporate agreement which will command general acceptance; and partly because serious problems are raised by the eighteenth-century history of the Panth. The first of these difficulties must await our discussion of authority in a later chapter. It is the second of them which demands our attention at this stage.

Inevitably it has been assumed that the essence and substance of the Rahit must have been determined by Guru Gobind Singh during his own lifetime, and that in communicating the Rahit to his Sikhs he was effectively promulgating a definitive version. A large portion would have been delivered on the occasion of the founding of the Khalsa in 1699 and the remainder would have been added shortly before his death. One of

[26] *Sikh Rahit Maryādā*, p. 28.

the extant rahit-namas reinforces this impression by purporting to record words spoken by the Guru during his stay in Abchalnagar immediately before he died.[27]

It is the rahit-namas themselves which prevent us from accepting this traditional schema. The tradition demands consistency, a pattern which demonstrably derives from the actual utterances of the tenth Guru and which is thereafter transmitted through succeeding generations in a regular and unambiguous form. This is not the pattern which the early rahit-namas deliver. They constitute a very considerable problem, one which must be solved with reasonable certainty if we are to achieve a satisfactory understanding of the eighteenth-century notion of Khalsa identity.

The best of our early sources is not a formal rahit-nama, but it deserves to be included in any such discussion because it incorporates a portion which briefly describes the requirements of the Rahit. This is Sainapati's *Gur Sobhā*, 'The Radiance of the Guru'. As its title indicates, this work proclaims the marvels of the Guru's glory. It is actually an early example of the gur-bilas or 'splendour of the Guru' style which acquired a dominant popularity during the eighteenth and nineteenth centuries, and, because it is relatively close to the tenth Guru himself, it is a very important source indeed. It is also important for the brief rahit-nama which it supplies and no adequate discussion of the early Rahit can avoid reference to it.[28]

Gur Sobhā nevertheless fails to satisfy the need for a comprehensive statement of the Rahit, one which can be unequivocally traced to the actual utterances of the Guru. This is partly because Sainapati had a larger purpose, setting his brief exposition of the Rahit within his denunciation of the arrogant and corrupt masands. More particularly it is because the actual date of the work has not yet been conclusively determined. The two contending dates are 1711 and 1745. If the first of these can be definitively established, there will be a significant strengthening of the rahit-nama sequence.[29] As far as specific identity injunctions are concerned, two come through with particular force in Sainapati's version of the Rahit. Predictably they are the ban on hair-cutting and condemnation of the hookah.[30]

---

[27] Piara Singh Padam (samp.), *Rahit-nāme* (Patiala, 1974), 53.

[28] Ganda Singh (samp.), *Kavī Saināpati rachit Srī Gur Sobhā*. For the gur-bilas literature, see McLeod (trans.), *Textual Sources for the Study of Sikhism*, pp. 11–13.

[29] Ganda Singh (samp.), *Kavī Saināpati rachit Srī Gur Sobhā*, pp. 21–3 (roman pagination).

[30] Ibid. 5: 19, 5: 21, 5: 24, 5: 30, pp. 22–4 (Gurmukhi pagination).

The examples of formal rahit-nama style which usually attract attention first are four brief poems. These relate, in simple Punjabi verse, conversations which their authors allegedly had with Guru Gobind Singh prior to his death. Two of them are attributed to Nand Lal (*Tanakhāh-nāmā* and *Prasan-uttar*). A third is attributed to a Sikh variously called Prahilad Singh or Prahilad Rai; and the fourth to Desa Singh, a resident of Amritsar who claims to have obtained his information from the Guru and from Nand Lal. The Nand Lal of the rahit-namas is obviously intended to be Bhai Nand Lal, a celebrated member of the tenth Guru's entourage and one renowned for his Persian poetry. There also exists a brief prose rahit-nama attributed to him. With the same cluster we can also associate the brief prose rahit-nama attributed to Daya Singh (one of the five Sikhs traditionally believed to have offered their heads at the inauguration of the Khalsa in 1699).[31]

There can be no doubt concerning the importance of these six brief works in the history of Sikh doctrine (especially doctrine relating to the Rahit and thus to the nature of the Khalsa). Their significance in this regard is well illustrated by the repeated use which Bhai Jodh Singh makes of them in the relevant chapter of his influential study of Sikh doctrine entitled *Guramati niraṇay*.[32] It is also indicated by some very familiar expressions. From where do the words *savā lakh* and *rāj karegā khālsā* come? They are to be found in the *Tanakhāh-nāmā*.[33] And where do we first encounter such expressions as *gurū khālsā māniahi, paragaṭ gurū kī deh* ('Accept the Khalsa as Guru, for it is the manifest body of the Guru') or *sabh sikhan ko bachan hai, gurū māniahu granth* ('Every Sikh is bidden to accept the Granth as Guru')? These lines we find in the rahit-nama attributed to Prahilad Singh.[34] They are accordingly works which should be treated with great respect.

Unfortunately they are also works which the historian has to treat with great reserve. This is because it is still impossible to identify them in terms of author, place, or time. The authorship of such figures as Nand Lal and Daya Singh must be rejected and so too must the claims which each rahit-nama makes to immediate contact with the Guru himself. The distinguished Bhai Nand Lal Goya could never have written the kind of

---

[31] For texts of these six brief rahit-namas, see Piara Singh Padam (samp.), *Rahit-nāme*, pp. 42–67, 134–45. For a text and translation of the prose rahit-nama attributed to Nand Lal, see McLeod (trans.), *The Chaupā Siṅgh Rahit-nāmā*, pp. 133–8, 202–4. It first appears attached to the much longer *Chaupā Siṅgh Rahit-nāmā*.

[32] Jodh Singh, *Guramati niraṇay* (Ludhiana, n.d.; 1st edn. 1932). chap. 14.

[33] Piara Singh Padam (samp.), *Rahit-nāme*, 34 and 36, p. 47.

[34] Ibid. 24 and 30, p. 55.

verse which these rahit-namas offer, and in all cases the language indicates a significant remove from the Guru's own time and environment. There are, moreover, some conspicuous errors, such as Prahilad Singh's claim that he received his instruction from the Guru in 1696.[35] Had he received it in Abchalnagar (as he specifically claims) he should have supplied a date corresponding to 1708.

Such features separate this cluster of rahit-namas from immediate contact with Guru Gobind Singh, but we must take care not to exaggerate the distance. Other features indicate a relatively early date. The most important of these is the impression which these rahit-namas give of a Rahit still in the process of formulation. Although we may have to detach them from the person and period of Guru Gobind Singh, this does not necessarily mean that we shall have to advance them well into the eighteenth century or the early nineteenth century.

We have here summarized a very intricate problem, one which still awaits a satisfactory determination. Part of our problem derives from the lack of early manuscript evidence. In its absence we shall have to depend upon analysis of language and content, an analysis which has yet to be adequately performed. A reasonable hypothesis seems to be an origin located somewhere in the middle decades of the eighteenth century. In the meantime, however, it remains a hypothesis.

Fortunately the same does not apply to the only lengthy rahit-nama which belongs to the eighteenth century. This is the prose rahit-nama attributed to Chaupa Singh Chhibbar, tutor to the infant Guru Gobind Singh and later one of his trusted advisers. An analysis of the *Chaupā Siṅgh Rahit-nāmā* indicates that it was compiled in its present form during the middle decades of the eighteenth century (between 1740 and 1765) and that it is accordingly the earliest of the datable rahit-namas. In its extant form it is a composite product mixing sections of classic rahit-nama material with anecdotes concerning Guru Gobind Singh, denunciation of the current Khalsa leadership, prophecies of imminent disaster, and a promise of ultimate glory.[36]

The composite nature of the *Chaupā Siṅgh Rahit-nāmā* points clearly to earlier sources and it is conceivable that portions of it may indeed go back to Chaupa Singh Chhibbar of the tenth Guru's entourage. These portions are impossible to identify with any certainty, although some parts can be safely detached from the rahit-nama's putative author and

[35] Ibid. 38, p. 56.
[36] McLeod (trans.), *The Chaupā Siṅgh Rahit-nāmā*, explains these in greater detail, pp. 24–8.

firmly located in a later period. The rahit-nama must be read as a mid-century interpretation of the Khalsa and its duty, as perceived by a particular family of Chhibbar Brahmans, once influential in the Panth but now pushed aside by coarsely aggressive successors.[37]

This firm identification is the basis of the rahit-nama's value today. Portions of its prolific content can be offensive to a modern Khalsa taste and it is easy to identify features which have made it an object of deep suspicion in orthodox circles. Notable in this respect is its claim that Brahmans are entitled to a special consideration in the Panth, a view which is unlikely to commend the source to those who support an egalitarian interpretation of the Panth.[38] Such features are nevertheless very valuable, for they sustain the credibility of the rahit-nama as a Chhibbar product and enable us to set it within a clearly definable context. Its profusion of detailed Rahit injunctions can thus be tagged in terms of source and period, and once this has been done the injunctions can be interpreted accordingly.

Although the Chhibbar connection arouses orthodox suspicions, it should not be assumed that these suspicions are necessarily valid. It does not follow that the rahit-nama will be unrepresentative or untrustworthy simply because of its Brahman provenance. On the contrary, the connection should considerably strengthen its claims, for this particular family had been very close to the tenth Guru and it can be plausibly maintained that for this very reason the rahit-nama deserves sympathetic analysis. The claim is strengthened by features which one might not have expected from a Brahmanic source. Strong emphasis is laid on the prime significance of the sword, on the role of the Khalsa Sikh as a soldier, and on the menace posed by polluting Muslims.[39]

Because the Rahit portions of the *Chaupā Singh Rahit-nāmā* are so lengthy and detailed, it is impossible to summarize them here.[40] There are two such sections, one specifying duties which the loyal Khalsa must perform and the other listing offences which require a penance (*tana-khāh*).[41] In addition to their many injunctions concerning warfare and the sword, the two lists include such predictable items as rules for harmonious relations within a sangat, appropriate rituals, reverence for the sacred scripture, various means of avoiding pollution, and an

---

[37] Ibid. 16–19.
[38] Ibid., section 24, p. 151.
[39] Ibid. 40, 42.
[40] The injunctions are summarized in ibid. 32–43.
[41] Ibid. 149–66, 174–90.

insistent stress on maintaining the hair uncut. Practices to be strictly avoided include smoking a hookah and eating *halāl* meat.

The *Chaupā Siṅgh Rahit-nāmā* thus incorporates the customary stress on the *kes* (the uncut hair), but it does not include the Five Ks (the *pañj kakke* or *pañj kakār*). The earliest extant version omits them altogether, and when a later version introduces a fivefold cluster, the actual items which it lists do not correspond to the *pañj kakke*. Three of the Five Ks are included (*kachh*, *kirpān*, and *kes*) but two are missing (*kaṅghā* and *kaṛā*). In their place we find *bāṇī* (the Gurus' utterances as recorded in sacred scripture) and *sādh saṅgat* (the fellowship of the devout).[42] Precisely the same situation is presented by the brief rahit-namas which we have tentatively assigned to the mid-eighteenth century. There too we find no reference to the *pañj kakke* in the early versions, though a reference subsequently appears in a later text of the *Prahilād Siṅgh Rahit-nāmā*.[43]

This particular instance can be generalized in the sense that other features of the orthodox Rahit as understood today are absent from the eighteenth-century evidence or are present as prototypes which have yet to attain firm definition. Others possess a clear definition, but their content or emphasis is subsequently amended in response to changing circumstances. From this evidence we must draw the following conclusion. A version of the Rahit was certainly current during the lifetime of Guru Gobind Singh but that version must be regarded as a nucleus, not as the full-fledged twentieth-century Rahit. In the meantime (and particularly during the early and middle decades of the eighteenth century) a process of growth and development took place, one which had produced the essential lineaments of the modern Rahit by the end of the eighteenth century.

This process of change and development continued through the nineteenth century into the twentieth and it still continues today. The Rahit

---

[42] Ibid., section 7a, p. 150.

[43] The twentieth-century version of the *Prahilād Siṅgh Rahit-nāmā* has an addendum attached which affirms the use of the *pañj kakke*. It appears in *Pothī rahit nāmā te tankhāh nāmā* (Amritsar, 1922), 16, and is quoted as authentic by Jodh Singh, *Guramati niraṇay*, p. 303.

> *kachh kes kaṅghā kirapān / kaṛā aur jo karau bakhān /*
> *ih kakke pañj tum māno / gurū granth sabh tum jāno /*

The portion is missing from Attar Singh's *The Rayhit Nama of Pralad Rai or the Excellent Conversation of Duswan Padsha and Nand Lal's Rayhit Nama or Rules for the Guidance of Sikhs in Religious Matters*, which was published from Lahore in 1876, and from earlier versions of the rahit-nama.

has never been static. It still responds to contemporary pressures, producing shifts in emphasis which gradually emerge as significant changes. Two interesting (and closely related) examples are provided by changing attitudes towards illicit sexual intercourse and towards Muslims.[44] If one compares modern injunctions with those from the eighteenth century, some interesting (yet unsurprising) differences become evident.

It thus appears that the developed Rahit must be ascribed to an extended period of evolution rather than limited to explicit pronouncements on the part of the tenth Guru. If this is indeed the case, it raises the question of how one identifies sources for the various elements included in the developed Rahit. Three general sources may be briefly postulated.

The first is the traditional source, namely the intention of the Gurus applied during the formative years of the Panth's growth and codified by Guru Gobind Singh as a nucleus of the later Rahit. This source delivered items relating to the importance of the sangat and to devotional practices designed to achieve *mukti* or spiritual liberation. Duties associated with the growing militancy of the Panth will also have developed during the course of the seventeenth century and we must also accept that an outward identity had been defined by the end of the century. Given the insistent stress on the *kes* in all rahit-namas, we can assume that the dominant feature of this external identity was its insistence on uncut hair.

Militant conventions and uncut hair point to a second source. This comprises the culture and traditions of the caste group which was progressively moving towards ascendancy within the Panth, particularly after the founding of the Khalsa. This ascendancy had presumably been reached in numerical terms before the ending of the line of personal Gurus, and during the eighteenth century it was to assume a much larger connotation. The Jats have long been distinguished by their militant traditions and by the custom of retaining their hair uncut. The influence of these traditions evidently operated prior to the formal inauguration of the Khalsa, fusing with the purpose of Guru Gobind Singh and thus emerging as significant features of the Khalsa nucleus. During the course of the eighteenth century the same influence accelerated as Jat leadership assumed an increasingly high profile within the Panth.

The third source also affected the development of the Rahit during the

---

[44] Compare injunctions 10 and 396 of McLeod (trans.), *The Chaupā Siṅgh Rahit-nāmā*, pp. 150 and 180, with [44](3) of *Textual Sources for the Study of Sikhism*, p. 85. Injunctions aimed at relations with Muslims, common in the eighteenth and first half of the nineteenth century, are absent today. *The Chaupā Siṅgh Rahit-nāmā*, p. 42.

seventeenth century, growing significantly in influence during the eighteenth. This was the pressure of contemporary circumstances, specifically the experience of warfare against enemies who increasingly were identified as Muslims. These circumstances served to strengthen the influence of the Jat source in that they encouraged militancy within the Panth. They stand alone as the source of some notable eighteenth-century injunctions aimed clearly and directly at Muslims.

The Rahit must thus be viewed as an evolving system, one which began to emerge during the earliest days of the Nanak-panth. It thereafter continued to develop formally (in accordance with deliberate decisions) and informally (in response to internal influences and external pressures). The precise distribution of these factors cannot be determined, particularly as all three were intertwined to a considerable extent. It is, however, possible to identify the appearance of certain key items and to reconstruct a loose sequence. This should enable us to describe in general terms the nature of the Khalsa identity at the beginning of the eighteenth century; the pattern of development which progressively enlarged and consolidated the Rahit during the course of the eighteenth century; and the developed identity which the Khalsa carried forward into the nineteenth century.

In so doing we must take care to set this Khalsa identity within the context of the larger Panth, ever aware that, however dominant the Khalsa mode may sometimes seem, its boundaries have never coincided with those of the Panth as a whole. It all depends, of course, on one's point of view. For some strict members of the Khalsa the two sets of boundaries are indeed coterminous and those who fail to meet Khalsa requirements are *ipso facto* deregistered as Sikhs. Although no one has ever managed to isolate the strict or 'fundamentalist' sector of the Panth, there can be little doubt that it always constitutes a comparatively small minority. The majority consists of the liberal, the lax, and the ambivalent, all of whom would presumably acknowledge a Panth larger than the orthodox Khalsa.

This means that our basic problem will persist, emerging in each period and generation to frustrate the promise of easy definition which the Khalsa so insistently proffers. We must also remind ourselves that the problem of definition will not be confined to a simple distinction between loyal Khalsa on the one hand and clean-shaven Sahaj-dhari on the other. Punjabi society will not permit such an easy solution, particularly in the villages which are home to a majority of those who call themselves Sikhs. A major aspect of the practical problem is the willingness of many

Punjabis to merge identities which the academic and the devout would prefer to keep separate. We shall delude ourselves if we imagine otherwise, just as we so easily misunderstand Sikh society if we insist on keeping our normative categories carefully intact.

Those categories are nevertheless essential if our analysis is to proceed and the most important of them is unquestionably the Khalsa. In the chapter which follows we shall accordingly focus our attention on the development of the Khalsa.

The Khalsa in the Eighteenth Century

When Guru Gobind Singh stood before his assembled followers on Baisakhi Day 1699 what did he actually say and do? We have already indicated two appropriate responses to this question, one cautiously sceptical and the other more positive. The first is that tradition has obviously embellished the occasion and that an analysis of the early sources requires the historian to suspend judgement on much of the traditional detail. The second is that something very significant obviously did happen in 1699 and that it should be possible to describe, in very general terms, the distinctive identity which marked those Sikhs who elected to join the Guru's Khalsa.

In attempting to envisage this identity we must always remember that it involves both an inheritance from the past and a continuing development in the future. This point, previously stressed when discussing the Rahit, means that certain features of the Khalsa discipline derive from the earliest days of the Nanak-panth. Others subsequently emerged in response to cultural influences operating within the Panth's constituency or to the pressure of political circumstances during the course of the seventeenth-century. The incorporating of such features in the formalized Rahit of the early Khalsa should serve to remind us that the 1699 event is set within a pattern of growth and development, and that the antecedents of this pattern extend well into the past. We should also remember that major features of the pattern belong to the future, evolving in response to the complex of influences which affect the Panth after 1699.

This should never suggest, however, that the 1699 event was unimportant. There is no reason to doubt that a rite of baptism was introduced on that famous Baisakhi Day, and, if indeed such a decision was implemented by Guru Gobind Singh, it marks a very significant development indeed. It means that a formal discipline was enunciated, one which required an explicit act of allegiance from all who accepted Khalsa initiation as the proper expression of loyalty to the Guru and his Panth. The discipline itself might continue to develop and mutate, but

this has done nothing to diminish the conviction that Khalsa membership requires the outward observance of certain objective standards.
Because a non-Khalsa option remained available, it also means that the
Panth has ever since been compelled to grapple with the problem of
differing identities. There is no evidence which suggests that in 1699 a
choice was offered between Khalsa initiation and expulsion from the
Panth.

The features of the 1699 tradition which seem to survive critical
scrutiny are listed by Professor J. S. Grewal as follows:

That a considerable number of the Sikhs used to visit Anandpur at the time of
Baisakhi and that on the Baisakhi of 1699 many of the Sikhs were specially asked
to come, that *khaṇḍe kī pāhul* [sword-baptism] was administered to those who
were willing to become the Guru's *Khālsā* (though no exact figures are
mentioned anywhere), that a considerable number of people—the *brāhmans* and
khatrīs in particular—rejected the *pāhul*, that the *Khālsā* were required to wear
keshas [uncut hair] and arms, that they were required not to smoke, that the
appellation of 'Singh' came to be adopted by a large number of the *Khālsā*—all
this is there in the earliest evidence.[1]

The fact that these points are to be found in the earliest chronicles does
not necessarily mean that they were all introduced in 1699, nor does it
tell us which of them (if any) were informally observed prior to 1699. It
does, however, indicate that a 1699 introduction must be regarded as
very likely in all instances and it definitively establishes them as features
of the Rahit as observed in the early eighteenth century. Five such
features emerge. An initiation ceremony involving the use of a sword was
instituted; initiants were to keep their hair uncut; weapons were to be
worn as a matter of course; smoking the hookah was forbidden; and
many (though not necessarily all) who thus entered the Khalsa adopted
the name 'Singh'.

This defines the essential Rahit as it was evidently understood at the
beginning of the eighteenth century. The fact that Brahman and Khatri
Sikhs were conspicuous amongst those who declined to accept the new
order presumably means that the predominant response came from Jats,
accompanied by smaller numbers from artisan castes. This assumption is
certainly supported by later evidence[2] and arguably it is also
strengthened by the distinctly militant tenor of the new dispensation.

Beyond these features we move into conjecture, supporting any

---

[1] J. S. Grewal, *From Guru Nanak to Maharaja Ranjit Singh: Essays in Sikh History*
(Amritsar, 1972), 59.

[2] See above, p. 21.

proposal which we may offer with whatever evidence may be available from later sources. One range of conjecture concerns the continuing Nanak-panthi tradition, those members of the Panth who declined *pāhul* (Khalsa initiation) and came to be known as Sahaj-dhari Sikhs. The term *sahaj-dhārī* was applied during the eighteenth century to Sikhs who cut their hair, and it is used in precisely this sense by the *Chaupā Siṅgh Rahit-nāmā*.[3] The word *sahaj* can mean 'slow' or 'natural', and *sahaj-dhārī* was subsequently construed to mean 'slow-adopter' or 'a Sikh who is still on the path to full Khalsa membership'. This, however, represents the strained interpretation of a later generation, one which is unlikely to be correct. A much more plausible etymology associates the term with Guru Nanak's use of *sahaj* to designate the condition of ultimate spiritual bliss which climaxes the *nām simaraṇ* technique. Those who emphasized Guru Nanak's interior practice of *nām simaraṇ* as opposed to the outward symbols of the new Khalsa identity would thus come to be known as 'those who affirm *sahaj*', or Sahaj-dhari Sikhs.[4]

The continuing presence of such Sikhs is plainly indicated by the testimony of the *B40 Janam-sākhī*. In this work, completed in 1733, we are offered clear evidence of a Nanak-panthi sangat living somewhere in the Gujranwala or Gujrat area. A prominent member of the sangat (the patron responsible for the recording of the janam-sakhi) is a Khatri called Daya Ram Abrol.[5] Nowhere in the entire work is there any hint of a Khalsa awareness, nor of the military struggles in which the Khalsa was so deeply involved. Indeed, there is an evident willingness to accept without demur that most heinous of Khalsa sins, the cutting of hair. In one anecdote an impoverished Sikh cuts and sells his hair in order to purchase food for the Guru.[6]

It is thus evident that those who declined to accept pahul continued to live as Nanak-panthi Sikhs, loyal to their original inheritance. As such they continued to regard themselves as Sikhs, sustaining an identity which was much less precise than that of the baptised Khalsa. The non-Khalsa constituency presumably included Kes-dhari Sikhs, those who retained their hair uncut without actually taking pahul. In terms of identity such Sikhs would be associated with the Amrit-dhari (the Sikh who had formally taken pahul) rather than with the arche-typal Sahaj-dhari who outwardly is indistinguishable from his or her

[3] W. H. McLeod (trans.), *The Chaupā Siṅgh Rahit-nāmā* (Dunedin, 1987), section 53, p. 154. Note, however, that his facial hair must be left untouched. See section 287, p. 176.
[4] McLeod, *Early Sikh Tradition: A Study of the Janam-sākhīs* (Oxford, 1980), 35 n.
[5] McLeod (trans.), *The B40 Janam-sākhī* (Amritsar, 1980), intro. pp. 19–25.
[6] Ibid., text p. 50. Id., *Early Sikh Tradition*, pp. 264–5.

Hindu neighbour. For some the choice would have reflected genuine convictions, and we must accept that this would apply to many of the Khatris and Brahmans who declined to accept initiation. For others it would presumably depend on circumstances. Periods of persecution would favour a discreet shedding of Khalsa symbols (particularly the *kes*), thereby producing a Sahaj-dhari identity. Khalsa success, by contrast, would favour a resumption of the symbols and a resurgence of the Kes-dhari identity.[7]

The Sahaj-dhari presence must always be kept in mind as we proceed through the eighteenth century, and likewise the existence of other identities which might claim an affiliation with the larger Panth. One which raises particular difficulties is the Udasi sect, an ascetic tradition claiming descent from Guru Nanak's elder son Siri Chand. The Udasi sect is distinguished by practices which clearly relate it to the Nath tradition, and, given Nanak's firm rejection of Nath practices, the Udasis should probably be set outside the Panth. The reputed descent from Siri Chand, aided by later connections of a distinctly tenuous nature, has nevertheless sustained an uncertain affiliation.[8] This was subsequently strengthened to some extent by the fact that during the eighteenth and nineteenth centuries many gurdwaras were maintained by individuals and lineages identified as Udasis. Although they are said to have been recognized by the later Gurus, they remain an obscure group, yet another of the many instances where uncertain tradition does service for established fact.[9]

In terms of visibility and participation in the Panth's evolving traditions, groups such as the Udasis are at one extreme. Sahaj-dharis are scarcely more prominent. Throughout the eighteenth century it is the Khalsa which occupies the stage, conspicuously dominant in all that passes as Sikh history and easily communicating the impression that all such history is in fact Khalsa history. This is not surprising. It is a development which can be easily understood in the light of political circumstances in eighteenth-century Punjab and in terms of the vigorous manner in which members of the Khalsa respond to those circumstances.

[7] Khushwant Singh, *A History of the Sikhs*, i (Princeton, 1963), 120. Teja Singh and Ganda Singh, *A Short History of the Sikhs* (Bombay, 1950), 110.

[8] The most significant of the Udasi connections with the orthodox Panth was the adherence to Udasi ideals of Baba Gurditta, eldest son of Guru Hargobind. Later Sikh tradition represents this allegiance as the route whereby Siri Chand eventually acknowledged the legitimate line of Gurus. Teja Singh, *Sikhism: Its Ideals and Institutions* (1938; rev. edn., Calcutta, 1951), 63.

[9] The Udasi panth is dealt with by Sulakhan Singh, 'The Udasis under Sikh Rule' (unpub. Ph.D. thesis, Guru Nanak Dev University, Amritsar, 1985). See also Teja Singh, *Sikhism*, pp. 58–66.

Uncertainty was followed by persecution, and persecution by counterattack. The counter-attack proved to be increasingly successful and eventually resulted in armed bands of Khalsa Sikhs dominating much of the Punjab. This in turn led to internecine warfare, but unity was finally imposed by the Sikh leader Ranjit Singh and the eighteenth century closed with the effective establishment of his rule over most of the Punjab.[10]

In sketching the history of the Panth during the eighteenth century a special kind of caution is needed. Inevitably and quite properly we focus much of our attention on the chronic warfare of the period, and in dealing with the various participants we necessarily give prominence to Mughals and Afghans on one side and the Khalsa Sikhs on the other. In so doing we can easily fall victim to the compelling strength of Khalsa historiography, presenting a view of the period which essentially depends on the themes and assumptions of that interpretation. Let no one underestimate its seductive power. This is the heroic period of Sikh tradition and its vibrant appeal can be very difficult to resist if one is predisposed to favour the Sikh cause. For those who are hostile to their cause the result is liable to be a comprehensive rejection of the tradition or a condemnation of what can easily be represented as bloody and uncouth. The tradition delivers a historiography and a mythology which tend strongly to polarize opinion. Although historians should be well aware of such a possibility, they are not necessarily immune from its extrovert charms or its subtle fascination.[11]

The warning to historians and their readers is, of course, a comment on the strength of the Khalsa ideal, a tribute to the influence which it exercises on those who subscribe to it as a belief and as a way of life. The fact that the heroic ideal has achieved such an ascendancy tells us something very important about Sikh identity, a message which powerfully reinforces Khalsa claims to represent all that is right and true in the teachings of the Gurus. *Here*, it insists, are the authentic traditions of the Panth. Others may perceive and practise vital aspects of the Gurus' message, but only in the Khalsa ideal does one find the fullness and the fulfilment of what Guru Gobind Singh intended his followers to be.

In thus emphasizing the strength of this tradition we will normally be referring to the modern Panth and to beliefs which exercise a considerable influence today. Their contemporary relevance is a basic fact which

---

[10] J. S. Grewal, *The Sikhs of the Punjab* (Cambridge, forthcoming), chap. 5.

[11] This tradition informs the interpretation of Khushwant Singh, *A History of the Sikhs*, i, chaps. 7–11. In Teja Singh and Ganda Singh, *A Short History of the Sikhs*, pt. III, it is considerably more pronounced.

should certainly be acknowledged and it is one to which we shall return when we deal with the Panth in the late twentieth century. Here, however, our primary concern must be with the generating of the tradition, with the events which supply its content, and with the early interpretations which produce its distinctive mould. We are still in the eighteenth century and at this point we are concerned with the developing consciousness which accompanied Khalsa involvement in the unfolding events of the century.

It was an involvement which began in defeat and uncertainty. Guru Gobind Singh himself fought wars which a detached observer would regard as defeats, although we must also heed the interpretation which transforms these events by stressing the heroism and inflexible determination of the Guru. Uncertainty followed with Banda Bahadur, leader of the uprising which created a disturbance in the Punjab between 1709, and his capture by Mughal troops at the end of 1715. Although Banda has long since been incorporated within Khalsa tradition as one who loyally upheld its finest ideals, the contemporary situation was probably rather more ambiguous. There were evidently disputes between Banda and his immediate followers on the one hand and the so-called Tat Khalsa (the 'True Khalsa') on the other.[12] These disputes, which concerned the proper form of Khalsa observances, should come as no surprise. The Khalsa had been in existence barely fifteen years when disagreement first developed between the Bandai Khalsa and the Tat Khalsa, a period much too brief for clear definition to have emerged on all significant points.

As we have already observed when discussing the Rahit, it was a definition which developed during the course of the decades which followed. In so doing it reflected the circumstances encountered by the Khalsa, specifically the experience of warfare. For several years after Banda's capture and execution this involved a desperate defence against intermittent campaigns to destroy their influence, campaigns which are represented in Sikh tradition as attempts by vicious Mughal authorities to exterminate the Khalsa completely.[13] Names such as Zakarya Khan, Lakhpat Rai, and Mir Mannu figure prominently in Khalsa demonology and are still invoked today as examples of the kind of fierce enemy whom Sikhs must resist whenever they appear.

---

[12] Khushwant Singh, *A History of the Sikhs*, i. 121–2. Teja Singh and Ganda Singh, *A Short History of the Sikhs*, pp. 111–16. G. S. Chhabra, *Advanced History of the Punjab*, i (rev. edn., Jullundur, 1968), 344.

[13] Gopal Singh, *A History of the Sikh People 1469–1978* (New Delhi, 1979), ch. xv.

After Ahmad Shah Abdali began his long series of invasions in 1747, Mughals were replaced by Afghans as the principal persecutor and foe, but the essential pattern remains unchanged. It includes calamities such as the Lesser Disaster (*Chhoṭā Ghalūgārā*) of 1746 and the Great Disaster (*Vāḍā Ghalūgārā*) of 1762. Another important feature is martyrdom, a prominent example being the cruel execution in 1738 of the deeply revered Mani Singh. Throughout the entire period the tradition carries tales of heroism, stories of dedicated Sikhs of the Khalsa who expressed their faith and loyalty in determined resistance to the forces of tyranny and destruction.[14]

The figure who pre-eminently draws these themes together in a single episode is that most famous of all Sikh martyrs, Baba Dip Singh Shahid. Dip Singh, a Jat from Lahore district and a trusted follower of Guru Gobind Singh, had fought with Banda and had subsequently become one of the principal leaders of the Khalsa resistance. In 1757, after Afghan invaders had desecrated Harimandir (now commonly known as the Golden Temple), Dip Singh took a solemn vow to enter Amritsar and there endeavour to repossess the ruined temple. Near Tarn Taran his force was confronted by a large Afghan army and Dip Singh met a fate variously described in popular Sikh tradition. According to the dominant version his head was cut off, but clutching it with one hand he continued to fight his way forward for another fifteen kilometres before succumbing to his injury within the bounds of Amritsar.[15] A distinctly gory picture of the decapitated Dip Singh is perhaps the most popular of the coloured prints available today in the bazaars of the Punjab and Delhi.[16]

A significant detail in the Dip Singh tradition concerns the desecration of Harimandir. This was, of course, perpetrated by Muslims and it is believed to have included the dumping of cows' entrails into the sacred pool. Hostility towards Muslims is another of the themes illustrated by the martyrdom of Dip Singh, a theme which finds clear expression in the early rahit-namas.[17] Muslims can never be trusted, their touch will pollute, and Sikhs are required to avoid their company at all times.[18] If necessary the sword must be used against Muslims, for it is they who threaten *dharma*.

This, it should be noted, is not a message communicated by the janam-

---

[14] Harbans Singh, *The Heritage of the Sikhs* (New Delhi, 1983), chaps. viii and ix.
[15] Gian Singh, *Tavārīkh Gurū Khālsā* (2nd edn., Patiala, 1970), ii. 198–9. Teja Singh and Ganda Singh, *A Short History of the Sikhs*, p. 155.
[16] The picture appears in W. H. McLeod, *Popular Sikh Art* (New Delhi, forthcoming).
[17] McLeod, *The Chaupā Siṅgh Rahit-nāmā*, intro. p. 42.
[18] Ibid., injunctions 10, 31, 120, and 442, pp. 150, 152, 160, 183.

sakhis. In the janam-sakhis we find Guru Nanak portrayed as the conciliator of Hindu and Muslim. It is true that they often portray him as one who rebukes bigoted qazis and if necessary humbles them; and it is also true that the janam-sakhis develop their own distinctive 'Triumph over Islam' theme.[19] Their criticisms of Muslims and Muslim doctrine are, however, comparatively muted and they are accompanied by a 'Nanak the Unifier' theme, so effectively portrayed in the regular presence of the Hindu Bala and the Muslim Mardana.[20]

In this regard the rahit-namas differ dramatically from the janam-sakhis, and they also run counter to the philosophy of Guru Gobind Singh himself. A celebrated passage from *Akāl Ustat* declares that 'mankind is one, that all men belong to a single humanity',[21] and in the lines which follow it specifically relates this belief to the relationship between Hindu and Muslim. The rahit-namas put their emphasis else-where. Faithfully reflecting attitudes developed during the eighteenth century and possibly earlier, the more outspoken of the rahit-namas identify the Muslim as the enemy and record injunctions which express this conviction. A later generation of Sikhs, reared in different circum-stances, was to perceive the issue differently and so to return to the janam-sakhi interpretation. For the eighteenth-century Khalsa, however, the enemy was typically a Muslim or the servant of Muslims. As a result Muslims as such were to be treated with wary caution or open hostility.

The enemies of the Khalsa, dominant at first and a continuing threat for most of the century, were eventually overcome. During the period of struggle the Khalsa looked forward to this ultimate triumph and at some point its confident expectation found expression in the triumphant words *rāj karegā khālsā*, 'the Khalsa shall rule'.

> The Khalsa shall rule, no enemy shall remain.
> All who endure suffering and privation shall be brought to the safety of the Guru's protection.[22]

Here we have another example of an eighteenth-century attitude requiring reinterpretation for a later generation. The eighteenth-century understanding, however, needs no such gloss. The Khalsa was involved in a struggle, first for survival and then for control. Through early defeat and later victory it moved steadily towards military triumph and political power, eventually securing the objective which destiny decreed. For

---

[19] McLeod, *Early Sikh Tradition*, pp. 255–6.
[20] Ibid. 172–3, 255.
[21] Dasam Granth, p. 19.
[22] Piara Singh Padam (samp.), *Rahit-nāme* (Patiala, 1974), 47.

many the climax and authentic fulfilment of the promise was to be the kingdom of Maharaja Ranjit Singh, established at the turn of the century.

The heroic ideals which thus developed during the course of the eighteenth century found expression in a variety of literature distinct from the rahit-namas. Reference has already been made to Sainapati's *Gur Sobhā* as the earliest example of the gur-bilas or 'splendour of the Guru' style.[23] Works which follow this style concentrate on the lives of the Gurus rather than on the events of the eighteenth century, but their treatment clearly reflects the ideals of the later period within which the style was developed. An obvious antecedent is supplied by *Bachitar Nāṭak*, an account of Guru Gobind Singh's early life which is attributed to the Guru himself. In *Bachitar Nāṭak* we find the same sense of destiny that characterizes the gur-bilas literature, the same emphasis on the paramount need to uphold *dharma* and on the obligation to use the sword in its defence if evil men persist in attacking it.[24]

Another eighteenth-century example of the standard form is Sukha Singh's *Gur-bilās Dasvīn Pātśāhī*, followed in the first half of the nineteenth century by Ratan Singh Bhangu's *Prāchīn Panth Prakāś*. Most of the gur-bilas literature actually belongs to the nineteenth century, sustaining through to the twentieth century a style and an interpretation which took shape within the Khalsa during the struggles of its heroic period. Some of its products have been extensively mined as sources for Sikh history, commonly without due regard for the date of composition or for the interpretation which so graphically informs them.[25]

It is when due allowance is made for these features that they yield their principal contribution. Examples of gur-bilas literature, like the rahit-namas, should be read primarily as works which reflect an unfolding perception of the mission of Guru Gobind Singh and of the divinely appointed role of the Khalsa. It is certainly not safe to assume that a particular incident or doctrine can be attached to the historical Guru Gobind Singh simply because it is so recorded in any or all of these works. We can, however, use them in our attempt to trace the development of convictions and attitudes which find expression in such references.

---

[23] See above, p. 35.

[24] Surjit Singh Hans, 'Historical Analysis of Sikh Literature, AD 1500–1850' (unpub. Ph.D. thesis, Guru Nanak Dev University, Amritsar, 1980), fos. 371–82, 392. Id., 'Social Transformation and the Creative Imagination in Sikhism' in Sudhir Chandra (ed.), *Social Transformation and Creative Imagination* (New Delhi, 1984), 99–101.

[25] W. H. McLeod, *The Sikhs: History, Religion and Society* (New York, 1989), chap. 6. Id. (trans.), *Textual Sources for the Study of Sikhism* (Manchester, 1984), 12.

A conspicuous example, one which concerns the fundamental belief structure of the Khalsa, is the doctrine of the eternal Guru. This doctrine, having emerged in the early Nanak-panth, is carried forward from the period of the personal Gurus into the eighteenth century and beyond. For Nanak the Guru was the 'voice' of Akal Purakh, mystically uttered within the inner being of the individual believer. Because Nanak comprehended the divine message and relayed it to his Sikhs, he became for them an actual embodiment of the eternal Guru. This same spirit passed onwards from each of the personal Gurus to his successor as a single flame passes from one torch to another. Guru Gobind Singh, however, died without a successor.[26] What happened thereafter to the eternal Guru?

The orthodox doctrine affirms that Guru Gobind Singh, immediately prior to his death in 1708, declared that after he had gone there would be no successor as personal Guru. The eternal Guru would remain with his followers, mystically present in the sacred scripture and in the gathered community. The scripture thus becomes the Guru Granth and the assembled community becomes the Guru Panth.

Two early sources are commonly cited in support of the traditional doctrine and its formal delivery by Guru Gobind Singh. The first is Sainapati's *Gur Sobhā*.

On an earlier occasion the Guru had been approached by his Sikhs and had been asked what form the [eternal] Guru would assume [after he had departed this earthly life]. He had replied that it would be the Khalsa. 'The Khalsa is now the focus of all my hopes and desires,' he had declared. 'Upon the Khalsa which I have created I shall bestow the succession. The Khalsa is my physical form and I am one with the Khalsa. To all eternity I shall be manifest in the Khalsa. They whose hearts are purged of falsehood will be known as the true Khalsa; and the Khalsa, freed from error and illusion, will be my true Guru.

'And my true Guru, boundless and infinite, is the eternal Word, the Word of wisdom which the devout contemplate in their hearts, the Word which brings ineffable peace to all who utter it, the Word which is wisdom immeasurably unfolded, the Word which none may ever describe. This is the light which is given to you, the refuge of all who inhabit the world, and the abode of all who renounce it.'[27]

The second source is the *Prasan-uttar* attributed to Nand Lal.

[26] By the time of Gobind Singh the successor as Guru was always chosen from amongst the male lineage in the Guru's own family, normally the eldest son of the deceased Guru. All four of Guru Gobind Singh's sons had predeceased him.

[27] Sainapati, *Sri Gur Sobhā*, 8: 40–3. Ganda Singh edition, pp. 128–9.

The Guru speaks: 'Listen attentively, Nand Lal, and I shall explain. I am manifested in three ways: the formless or invisible (*nirguṇ*), the material or visible (*sarguṇ*), and the divine Word (*gur-śabad*) . . . The second is the sacred scripture, the Granth. This you must accept as an actual part of me, treating its letters as the hairs of my body. This truly is so.

'Sikhs who wish to see the Guru will do so when they come to the Granth. He who is wise will bathe at dawn and humbly approach the sacred scripture. Come with reverence and sit in my presence. Humbly bow and hear the words of the Guru Granth. Hear them with affection and alert attention. Hear the Guru's Word of wisdom and read it that others may also hear. He who wishes to converse with me should read or hear the Granth and reflect on what it says. He who wishes to hear any words should attentively read or hear the Granth. Acknowledge the Granth as my visible presence, rejecting the notion that it is other than me.

'The Sikh himself is the third form which I take, that Sikh who is forever heedful of the words of sacred scripture (*gurbāṇī*). He who loves and trusts the Word of the Guru is himself an ever-present manifestation of the Guru. Such a Sikh is the one who hears the Guru's words of wisdom and reads them so that others may hear. It is he who attentively recites both *Japjī* and *Jāp*, who regularly visits the gurdwara, and who strictly avoids adulterous liaisons. The Gursikh who is faithful in serving his Master will find himself cleansed from all sense of self-dependence. He who is scrupulous in performing these obligations is the Sikh in whom I am made manifest.'[28]

Both sources provide clear statements of the orthodox doctrine, or at least of versions which can be construed as consonant with the standard *Gurū Granth/Gurū Panth* interpretation. The doctrine is, moreover, one which is easily related to elements in the earlier Nanak-panth which plainly foreshadow it. Each personal Guru incarnated the eternal Guru, and, because the sacred volume contains the compositions (*bāṇī*) of the Gurus, it implicitly represents the spirit which each embodied. Guru Ram Das explicitly identifies *bāṇī* and *gurū*,[29] and from this declaration it is but a short step to the formulated doctrine of the scriptural Guru (the *Gurū Granth*). In like manner the *Gurū Panth* doctrine is foreshadowed in the early Gurus' emphasis on the divine quality of a satsang or an assembly of true believers. A couplet from Bhai Gurdas points forward to the developed doctrine:

> He who receives the Guru's teachings must live a life which reflects their truth.

---

[28] Piara Singh Padam (samp.), *Rahit-nāme*, pp. 42–3.
[29] Guru Ram Das, *Naṭ Aṣṭapadi* 4(5), Adi Granth, p. 982.

> Let him take his place in the company of the faithful, absorbing their
> virtue in the presence of the Word.[30]

The line of doctrinal development is logical and clear, easily accommodating the final version within the established tradition of the Nanak-
panth.[31]

There remain important questions, however, and these questions
require answers before the process can be fully understood or its place
within the Khalsa tradition satisfactorily determined. The first question
concerns the point in time at which the dual doctrine actually crystallized. Was it immediately prior to the tenth Guru's death or did it occur
later? Secondly, is the *Gurū Granth* doctrine confined to the Adi Granth
(a common assumption today) or does it also include the Dasam Granth?
Thirdly, is the expression *Gurū Panth* synonymous with *Gurū Khālsā* or
does it possess a wider application?

We can dispose of the second of these questions summarily, for there
appears to be no doubt concerning either the answer or its practical
effect. As far as the eighteenth-century Khalsa was concerned, the Dasam
Granth was as much a part of the canon as the Adi Granth.[32] The Dasam
Granth breathes a militant spirit which matches that of the eighteenth-
century Khalsa. Its influence on Khalsa ideals is well illustrated by
portions of the *Chaupā Siṅgh Rahit-nāmā* and by the strong fascination
exercised within the eighteenth-century Panth by the Devi cult.[33]

The answer to the first question is rather more complex. It depends to
some extent on the dating of *Gur Sobhā*, which, as we noted earlier, may
be either 1711 or 1745.[34] If the former is correct, and if the relevant
passage is demonstrably a part of the original text, the traditional
connection with Guru Gobind Singh will be very difficult to dispute. It
remains, however, one of the points on which we are compelled to
suspend judgement in the meantime. What we can affirm with certainty
is that the *Gurū Panth* doctrine performed a significant service to the
Khalsa during the middle decades of the eighteenth century. It is also
evident that a significant phase in the crystallizing process belongs to this
period, a phase which produced a practical expression of the doctrine
well suited to the contemporary needs of the Khalsa.

During the period of persecution and guerrilla warfare which followed

---

[30] *Vārān Bhāi Gurdās* 3: 9.   [31] McLeod, *Early Sikh Tradition*, p. 262.
[32] John Malcolm, 'Sketch of the Sikhs', *Asiatick Researches*, xi (Calcutta, 1810), 221,
255, 281. For the Dasam Granth, see McLeod, *The Sikhs*, chap. 6.
[33] McLeod (trans.), *The Chaupā Siṅgh Rahit-nāmā*, pp. 47, 172–3.
[34] See above, p. 35.

the execution of Banda, the Khalsa faced serious problems of co-ordinated strategy and organization. These derived partly from the absence of a single leader and partly from the scattering of Khalsa forces by its stronger enemies. For more than a decade following 1733 Kapur Singh was recognized as leader of the Khalsa, but the problem of con-solidating its forces persisted and other individuals continued to function as commanders of separate *jathā*s or warrior bands.[35]

Towards the middle of the century many of the jathas were consoli-dated into twelve groups of varying size, each known as a *miṣl*. Although this development marked a significant strengthening of Khalsa power, it also conferred a greater influence on individual misl commanders. Men such as Jassa Singh Ahluwalia and Jai Singh Kanaihya led independent armies. All acknowledged a common Khalsa loyalty and all confronted the same foe, but the possibilities of fraternal conflict were ever present and an effective understanding was needed if the various jathas and misls were to overcome its dangers.[36]

A significant part of the answer was supplied by the doctrine of the Guru Panth. It was one thing to agree that Khalsa spells brotherhood and that the scattered groups should accept membership in a single united army, the Dal Khalsa. It was quite another matter to sustain a degree of unity sufficient to convert a pious ideal into a practical reality. The doctrine of the Guru Panth contributed significantly to the solving of this problem in that the leaders of the various groups believed that their meetings were held in the presence of the Guru and that decisions reached under such circumstances represented the will of the Guru.[37]

This conviction was defined in precise terms as the doctrine of the gurumata, or 'the intention of the Guru'. During the period of the Afghan invasions there developed the practice of holding biannual assemblies of the Sarbat Khalsa (the 'Entire Khalsa') before Akal Takhat in Amritsar. These meetings were held in the presence of the Guru Granth Sahib and a formal decision reached after debate by the leaders of the misls was called a gurumata. As such it was held to represent the will of the eternal Guru and a refusal to accept any such resolution constituted rebellion against the Guru himself.[38]

The belief was particularly effective during the years covered by the Afghan invasions, a period marked by increasing Khalsa strength but not

[35] Surjit Singh Gandhi, *The Struggle of the Sikhs for Sovereignty* (Delhi, 1980), 66–8.

[36] Khushwant Singh, *A History of the Sikhs*, i. 131–3.

[37] Teja Singh and Ganda Singh, *A Short History of the Sikhs*, pp. 111–12.

[38] J. S. Grewal, 'The Rule of Law and Sikh Thought', *Journal of Sikh Studies*, 11/2 (Aug. 1984), 137.

by total security. As the Afghan threat receded and individual misls acquired a more secure power, the doctrine weakened and disagreement within the Khalsa became more acute. Its practical effect came to an end with the triumph of Ranjit Singh. Having progressively subdued the other sardars (the misl chieftains), Ranjit Singh was eventually proclaimed Maharaja of the Punjab in 1801 and a single administration was established over most of the area previously divided amongst the various chieftains. Ranjit Singh continued to rule in the name of the Khalsa, but gatherings of the Sarbat Khalsa were unlikely to meet with his approval.[39] The practice of holding such assemblies was allowed to lapse and the doctrine of the Guru Panth gradually atrophied. As it declined, the doctrine of the Guru Granth assumed a larger prominence, acquiring an influence which it retains to the present day.

One other eighteenth-century result of the dual doctrine concerns the development of the gurdwara as an institution. During the period of the Nanak-panth the Guru's followers assembled for kirtan in rooms or buildings called dharamsalas.[40] This practice continued throughout the eighteenth century and by the end of the century the place of assembly was still called a dharamsala.[41] Meanwhile, however, there had developed the custom of erecting shrines called gurdwaras. These evidently marked locations associated with particular events in the lives of individual Gurus, places to which a Sikh might make a pious pilgrimage.[42]

Eventually this latter usage was enlarged to include the dharamsala and it seems likely that it was the doctrine of the eternal Guru which produced the change.[43] It may have been because the sangat which gathered in a dharamsala represented the corporate Guru, or it may have resulted from the practice of installing copies of the sacred scripture (the Guru Granth) in the room which served as a dharamsala. The former is perhaps the more likely, for copies of the sacred scripture would have been too expensive for many sangats until the printing press eventually made them obtainable. If the latter is the dominant reason it presumably

---

[39] Narendra Krishna Sinha, *Ranjit Singh* (Calcutta, 1951), 137. See also J. S. Grewal, *The Reign of Maharaja Ranjit Singh* (Patiala, 1981), esp. pp. 4–5.

[40] McLeod, *Early Sikh Tradition*, pp. 261–2.

[41] Malcolm, 'Sketch of the Sikhs', p. 278.

[42] McLeod (trans.), *The Chaupā Singh Rahit-nāmā*, injunctions 111 and 120, pp. 159, 160. The word *gurduārā* (anglicized as 'gurdwara') can be translated either as 'by means of the Guru['s grace]' or as 'the Guru's door'.

[43] The use of the term in the *Praśan-uttar* attributed to Nand Lal suggests a later period in that it implies a much wider range of buildings than would have been covered by the early use of *gurduārā*. Piara Singh Padam (samp.), *Rahit-nāme*, p. 43.

means that the shift from dharamsala to gurdwara is comparatively recent.

There still remains the question of whether *Gurū Panth* and *Gurū Khālsā* are synonymous. In other words, is the voice of the eternal Guru uttered only in assemblies of the Sarbat Khalsa, or was it also accessible to Nanak-panthi sangats which lacked a Khalsa affiliation? There appears to be no doubt that Nanak-panthi sangats affirmed the doctrine and assumed the mystical presence of the Guru. This was certainly the view of the person responsible for the *B40 Janam-sākhī*: 'The sangat is the Court of the Supreme Guru and speaks as His voice. In your midst abides the supreme Guru and if any favour be asked of you [the sangat], it can be granted.'[44]

This response from the year 1733 is explicit, but it was not necessarily matched by assumptions developing within the Khalsa. We are confronted yet again by the persistent problem of the relationship between the Khalsa on the one hand and the Sahaj-dhari or Nanak-panthi Sikh on the other. During the course of the eighteenth century the difference became increasingly marked as the Khalsa tradition consolidated and political power passed into Khalsa hands. By the end of the century the Khalsa ideal was clearly dominant and to some foreign observers it seemed that all Sikhs were in fact Sikhs of the Khalsa.

Foreign observers provide us with some interesting and helpful commentaries on Sikh identity late in the eighteenth century and during the early years of the nineteenth. For the most part they seem to have been dependent on what they actually saw, and most of them were evidently unaware of the existence of Sikhs other than those who conspicuously displayed the symbols of the Khalsa tradition. The Sikhs whom they recognized were pre-eminently the troops of the Khalsa armies, flamboyant soldiers whom they admired for their riding skills and endurance while despising (or fearing) them for their loud voices and uncouth behaviour. Several such accounts derive from the last quarter of the eighteenth century and the first decade of the nineteenth, and together they present a reasonably consistent view of the Khalsa, as foreigners were able to observe it during that period. Although it was a partial view, based on an imperfect perception, it remains a useful one.[45]

---

[44] McLeod (trans.), *The B40 Janam-sākhī*, p. 241. Cf. also pp. 183, 198, 208.

[45] For these observers and their reports see Ganda Singh (ed.), *Early European Accounts of the Sikhs* (Calcutta, 1962). Ganda Singh's collection includes reports by Polier (1776 and c.1780), Wilkins (1781), Forster (1783), Browne (1787), Griffiths (1794), and Franklin (1803).

The various observations reported by these early European visitors can be consolidated as follows. The Sikhs whom they encountered late in the eighteenth century were impressive soldiers, particularly as horsemen.[46] Although the Sikhs admitted converts from all castes,[47] most were Jats[48] and very few came from Muslim origins (unless converted by force).[49] Following an initiation ceremony they refrained from cutting their hair,[50] wore an iron bangle on the wrist,[51] and clad themselves in dark-blue clothing with a prominent turban.[52] Smoking the hookah was strictly avoided, but not the free use of spirits, opium, and bhang.[53] They ate meat (including pork), but never touched beef.[54] A common utterance, frequently repeated, was 'Vah-gourou' (*Vāhigurū*).[55] The Swiss observer Colonel Polier notes the traditional antipathy towards Muslims;[56] and John Griffiths mentions the Khalsa assemblies held biannually in Amritsar, with the Guru Granth Sahib present on such occasions.[57]

One other passing reference which deserves to be noted is Polier's inclusion of 'a pair of blue drawers' as one of the few garments typically worn by the Sikhs whom he observed.[58] This, together with the uncut hair (*kes*) and bangle (*karā*), brings us very close to the Five Ks, for we can probably assume the sword (*kirpān*) as clearly implicit in their emphasis on weaponry and the comb (*kaṅghā*) would be concealed in the conspicuous turbans which they noted. It seems, however, that no one drew their attention to the actual convention as such. This, together with the absence of clear eighteenth-century rahit-nama testimony, may indicate that at the end of the century the convention was still emergent rather than clearly defined.

The impression thus communicated by late-eighteenth-century observers is considerably strengthened by the most important of all these

[46] Ganda Singh (ed.), *Early European Accounts of the Sikhs*, pp. 17, 25, 60, 81, 99.

[47] Ibid. 18, 56, 83, 92, 100.

[48] Ibid. 13, 56, 66. Griffiths and Franklin both drew specific attention to the connection which this feature established between Jats and Sikhs. Ibid. 88, 105.

[49] Ibid. 59, 83.

[50] Ibid. 18, 63, 65, 79, 92, 103–4.

[51] Ibid. 18, 63, 65, 66, 79, 105. Franklin notes that the bangles (like weapons) may be gold, silver, brass, or iron 'according to the circumstances of the wearers'. Ibid. 104–5.

[52] Ibid. 17, 63, 92, 100.

[53] Ibid. 18, 63, 65, 79, 104.

[54] Ibid. 63, 65, 92, 104.

[55] Ibid. 63, 65, 73.

[56] Ibid. 58–9.

[57] Ibid. 91. Griffiths's reference to 'their Ghiruntejee' does not indicate whether the Granth was the Adi Granth, the Dasam Granth, or both.

[58] Ibid. 93.

early European reports. In 1810 John Malcolm published his 'Sketch of the Sikhs', an account based on documents and information collected during a period spent in the Punjab in 1805.[59] Malcolm begins by describing Sikhs of the Khalsa as follows. 'The disciples of Govind were required to devote themselves to arms, always to have *steel* about them in some shape or other, to wear a blue dress, to allow their hair to grow, to exclaim when they met each other, *Wa! Guruji ka khalsah! Wa! Guruji ki futteh!*'[60] In the extended description which follows he largely confirms the reports of his earlier contemporaries as far as the outward identity of the Khalsa Sikh was concerned.[61] There are, however, two issues noted by Malcolm which deserve particular attention. One returns us to continuing distinctions within the Panth. The other concerns an evident awareness that Sikhs of the Khalsa were perceived as separate and distinct from Hindus.

The first of these contributions develops a point which had been mentioned in passing by his predecessor George Forster. In a letter written soon after his journey through the Punjab in 1783, Forster had briefly noted that all Sikhs were not 'Sings' of the 'military order'. There were also others, known as 'Khualasah Sikhs', who did not observe the outward forms of the Khalsa.[62] Malcolm deals with the distinction in greater detail. There are, he observes, several varieties of Sikhs, two of which deserve particular notice. First, and most assuredly foremost, there are the Khalsa Sikhs, easily identified by any casual observer. 'The character of the *Sikhs*, or rather *Sinhs*, which is the name by which the followers of Guru Govind, who are all devoted to arms, are distinguished, is very marked.'[63] This identity, he makes clear, is shared by 'the *Sikh* merchant, or cultivator of the soil, if he is a *Sinh*', not merely by the

---

[59] John Malcolm published his lengthy 'Sketch of the Sikhs' in 1810 in *Asiatick Researches*, xi. 197–292 (*Asiatick Researches: or Transactions of the Society Instituted in Bengal for enquiring into the History and Antiquities, the Arts, Sciences, and Literature of Asia*, Calcutta). It was subsequently issued as Lieutenant-Colonel Malcolm, *Sketch of the Sikhs, a Singular Nation, who inhabit the Provinces of the Penjab, Situated between the Rivers Jumna and Indus* (John Murray, London, 1812). All subsequent references to 'Sketch of the Sikhs' are from the 1810 edition in *Asiatick Researches*.

[60] Malcolm, 'Sketch of the Sikhs', p. 220.

[61] Malcolm describes the manner in which the Khalsa initiation was carried out. The initiant is required to 'allow his hair to grow', but the Five Ks (*pañj kakke*) are not mentioned. Instead 'five weapons' are presented to him (a sword, a firelock, a bow and arrow, and a pike). He is enjoined to avoid the company of 'men of five sects', though Malcolm's naming of them cannot be correct. Ibid. 285–7.

[62] George D. Forster, *A Journey from Bengal to England* (London, 1798), i. 266n, 268–9. The text presented by Ganda Singh omits this distinction.

[63] Malcolm, 'Sketch of the Sikhs', p. 259.

soldiers who so conspicuously paraded it.[64] The 'followers of Guru Govind' or Khalsa Sikhs are clearly distinguished by Malcolm from those whom he variously calls 'followers of Nanac' or 'Khalasa Sikhs' ('free' Sikhs, as opposed to those who abide by the Khalsa discipline).[65] The Khalasa Sikhs (Forster's 'Khualasah Sikhs') are of course, the Sahaj-dharis. Malcolm's prejudices show when he proceeds to describe them.

Their character differs widely from that of the *Sinhs*. Full of intrigue, pliant, versatile and insinuating, they have all the art of the lower classes of *Hindus*, who are usually employed in transacting business; from whom, indeed, as they have no distinction of dress, it is difficult to distinguish them.[66]

We may ignore the insult, but not the important reference to the lack of visible identity.

Malcolm's other important contribution follows from his observations on caste. Sikhs, he acknowledges, observe routine caste distinctions with regard to both marriage and dining (except at gatherings of the Sarbat Khalsa). In many instances, he notes, their caste-fellows regard them simply as 'Hindus that have joined a political association' and continue to have customary dealings with them.[67] This, he continues, was not in accordance with the intention of Guru Gobind Singh. The tenth Guru sought to demolish all distinctions of caste, thereby separating Sikhs from Hindus. The Guru's intention found expression in the initiation ceremony and (he claims) those who understand the meaning of that ceremony will appreciate that 'Guru Govind has separated his followers for ever from the Hindus'.[68]

This Khalsa sense of separation from Hindu society is confirmed by Ratan Singh Bhangu, author of *Prāchīn Panth Prakāś* and contemporary with Malcolm. Ratan Singh's argument runs as follows. Guru Gobind

[64] Ibid. 260.

[65] Ibid. 257, 260–1. In spite of the apparent similarity when written in the roman script, *khalāsā* and *khālsā* are two different words. The former had evidently dropped out of use by the middle of the nineteenth century. J. D. Cunningham, *A History of the Sikhs* (1st edn., London, 1849; rev. edn., Oxford, 1918), 90 n. Malcolm also notes the existence of Acalis, Shahids, Nirmalas, and Nanac Pautras ('Sketch of the Sikhs', pp. 261–2). The Acalis (Akalis) and Shahids are easily identified as particularly enthusiastic Khalsas; and the Nirmalas constituted an order of scholar Sikhs. The 'Nanac Pautra' are the 'descendants of Nanac' and thus presumably the same as the 'Nanac Putrah' (ibid. 201). Presumably they are thus to be identified as the Bedi descendants of Guru Nanak, a familial group which received veneration because of its distinguished origins (correctly descended from Lakhmi Das). Alternatively they are a variety of Khalasa Sikhs. Malcolm also refers to 'the sect of Udasi', founded by Nanak's son Dherm Chand (*recte* Siri Chand). Ibid. 200–1.

[66] Ibid. 261.

[67] Ibid. 262–3.

[68] Ibid. 288. See also pp. 269–70.

Singh, having vowed to destroy Muslim power, was confronted by the manifest weakness of his cowardly followers. The root of the problem, he decided, was the kind of meek initiation which they received as entrants to the Panth. In its place he would introduce the baptism of the sword, imbuing his followers with a spirit which would strike fear in the hearts of all whom they assailed. Each would take up his sword and each would adopt the martial name of Singh. The frontal mark, the sacred thread, and the despised dhoti would all be cast aside. Together the members of the recreated Panth would constitute a single caste, all eating from the same dish and all united in the same resolve.[69]

As we move into the nineteenth century we are left with the distinct impression of an ascendant Khalsa and of a Rahit approaching the form familiar to the twentieth century. It is true that the Five Ks are absent and indeed will still be absent in a formalized sense half a century later. The old enmity towards Muslims still survived, moreover, but for some at least another clear line of demarcation had been drawn. This new line was not one which distinguished Hindu from Sikh in terms which most would necessarily accept. It distinguished the Khalsa from all who adhered to Hindu forms, a distinction which set the Sahaj-dhari Sikh apart from the Khalsa and identified him with those whom everyone recognized as Hindu.

Others saw it differently. There were 'Sikhs of Nanac' and there were 'Sikhs of Govind', both members of the same Panth though differing in their understanding of what constituted true loyalty. One portion of the Panth had entered a powerful claim to orthodoxy and had evidently succeeded in convincing some observers of the justice of their claim. Others were less sure. Although the balance had swung strongly in one direction, the problem of defining the Panth still remained.

[69] Ratan Singh Bhangu, *Prāchīn Panth Prakāś* 16. Vir Singh edn. (Amritsar, 1962), 40–2.

5

The Singh Sabha Reformation

AT THE beginning of the nineteenth century stands the youthful Ranjit Singh, conqueror of Lahore and soon to be invested with the title of Maharaja. At its end we find the Singh Sabha movement approaching the peak of its influence. During the course of the century the Panth had experienced the triumphs of Ranjit Singh, the rapid decline of his successors, and defeat in two wars with the British. The conclusion of the second Anglo-Sikh War was followed by the final annexation of the Punjab in 1849 and by confident British forecasts of the imminent dissolution of the Panth.

The first Singh Sabha, or 'Singh Society', was established in 1873 and for several decades thereafter its reformist leaders preached reform and regeneration of the Khalsa. Acknowledging that the Panth was indeed under threat, they devised a programme of reform designed to restore the Khalsa traditions and loyalties which seemed so plainly to be eroding. Their success was impressive. By the time the movement began to fade early in the twentieth century a persuasive interpretation of Sikh tradition had been fashioned and the Khalsa identity had been defined with a precision never before achieved.[1]

When Ranjit Singh became Maharaja of the Punjab in 1801 it must have seemed to many a fulfilment of the *rāj karegā khālsā* prophecy, a final vindication of the eighteenth-century belief that the Khalsa would rule. That, certainly, has been the interpretation placed on those famous words by some twentieth-century Sikhs and most, it seems, look back on the four decades of Ranjit Singh's rule as something resembling a golden age. Ever since he achieved the conquest of the Punjab, Ranjit Singh has been regarded as a folk-hero, as one who embodied in his person and in his administration the ideals for which the Khalsa had fought during the preceding century.[2]

Inevitably there has developed a mythology associated with Ranjit Singh and, as with all such mythologies, its features reflect the

[1] Harbans Singh, *The Heritage of the Sikhs* (2nd rev. edn., New Delhi, 1983), 233, 259.
[2] Khushwant Singh, *A History of the Sikhs*, i (Princeton, 1963), 291–6.

aspirations of those for whom he had acquired symbolic significance. It is popularly believed, for example, that, although he ruled in the name of the Khalsa, he did so in a truly secular spirit. In this context 'secular' must be construed in its modern Indian sense as 'respecting all religions' and as such it is a prominent feature of the reputation which the late twentieth century attaches to Ranjit Singh.[3] If European observers are to be believed, the administration of Ranjit Singh was informed by the spirit and attitudes of the eighteenth century.[4] Individual Muslims were employed as state servants (some of them with considerable authority) but the eighteenth-century hostility towards Muslims had not been wholly exorcised from all areas of government nor from Sikh society in general.

It is upon the Khalsa identity of the administration that the emphasis must be laid, with the significant qualification that Ranjit Singh placed strict limitations on the earlier ideal of popular participation in decision-making. Loyal sardars were duly rewarded, but assemblies of the Sarbat Khalsa were no longer held and the institution of the gurumata was effectively suppressed. Substantial largesse was, however, bestowed on prominent Sikh shrines and at the Maharaja's court conspicuous respect was paid to the traditions of the Khalsa. Coinage bore the image of Guru Nanak, the administration was known as *Sarkār Khālsājī*, and the royal court itself was called *Darbār Khālsājī*.[5] There could be no doubting the importance attached to the reputation of the Khalsa or to the individual identity associated with it. In this sense the state administered by Ranjit Singh was an authentic extension of eighteenth-century Khalsa ideals.

This did not mean, however, that all Sikhs were satisfied with the attitudes and behaviour generated by military success or political patronage. From the period of Ranjit Singh date two reform movements which still command significant followings today. These are the original Nirankaris and the group variously known as Namdharis or as Kukas. Both are strictly sects, emerging within the larger Panth during the same period and in the same part of the Maharaja's domains. Both, moreover,

---

[3] Surinder Singh Johar, for example, has entitled his study of Maharaja Ranjit Singh *The Secular Maharaja* (Delhi, 1985).

[4] John Malcolm, 'Sketch of the Sikhs', *Asiatick Researches*, xi (Calcutta, 1810), 256–7. 'A Tour to Lahore (in 1808)' by an officer of the Bengal Army, *Asiatic Annual Register*, vol. xi for 1809, repr. in *The Panjab Past and Present*, 1/1 (Apr. 1967), 120. Alexander Burnes, *Travels into Bokhara* (London, 1834), iii. 118–19. G. T. Vigne, *Travels in Kashmir &c* (London, 1842), i. 184. Charles Masson, *Narratives of Various Journeys in Balochistan, Afghanistan, and the Panjab* (London, 1842), i. 409–10. Charles von Hugel, *Travels in Kashmir and Punjab* (London, 1845), 190–1, 238.

[5] Khushwant Singh, *A History of the Sikhs*, i. 201.

stand under much the same condemnation as far as strictly orthodox Sikhs are concerned, for each acknowledges a continuing line of Gurus. Because of these obvious similarities the two movements are commonly mentioned in the same breath, a convention which may suggest that their resemblances are more important than their differences. Any such impression is wholly misleading, particularly in the context of a discussion concerning the nineteenth-century development of Sikh identity.[6]

Nirankaris trace their origins as a distinctive group to Baba Dayal Das, a Khatri shopkeeper of Rawalpindi. Baba Dayal's following came to be known as Nirankaris because of the emphasis which he laid on the formless quality (*nirankār*) of Akal Purakh, the attribute which contrasted so strongly with the contemporary understanding of piety and religious duty. External observance, whether idol worship or visible symbols, could never achieve liberation. Only by returning to Nanak's exclusive stress on the interior discipline of *nām simaraṇ* could this be attained.

Baba Dayal was not a member of the Khalsa, nor were most of his early followers. The sect was strictly a Nanak-panthi movement, one which preached a return to the original teachings of Nanak without significant reference to the later traditions of the Khalsa. As a result of the Singh Sabha campaign later in the century, many Nirankaris did eventually adopt the Khalsa insignia. The Nirankari tradition nevertheless retained its Nanak-panthi philosophy and it continued to attract a substantial number of adherents who identified as Sahaj-dhari Sikhs, as Hindus, or as both.[7]

Although the Namdhari movement started in much the same way, it significantly changed its complexion under its second Guru. The founder was Balak Singh of Hazro and, like Baba Dayal, he lived his life in the

---

[6] The Nirankaris and Namdharis are covered in all the standard histories. See Harbans Singh, *The Heritage of the Sikhs*, chap. xvii; and W. H. McLeod (trans.), *Textual Sources for the Study of Sikhism* (Manchester, 1984), 13–14, 121–31. There are few studies concerning only the Nirankaris. See John C. B. Webster, *The Nirankari Sikhs* (Delhi, 1979). The Namdharis, or Kukas, have been rather better treated. See Fauja Singh Bajwa, *Kuka Movement* (Delhi, 1965). There are also five volumes of documents. Three of these have been edited by Nahar Singh under the title *Gooroo Ram Singh and the Kuka Sikhs* (New Delhi and Sri Jiwan Nagar, 1965–6); and two of them by Jaswinder Singh as *Kukas of Note in the Punjab* (Sri Bhaini Sahib, 1985) and *Kuka Movement* (New Delhi, 1985). See also the short study by Gurmit Singh, *Sant Khalsa* (Sirsa, 1978). For a brief account, see W. H. McLeod, 'The Kukas: A Millenarian Sect of the Punjab', in G. A. Wood and P. S. O'Connor, *W. P. Morrell: A Tribute* (Dunedin, 1973), 85–103; repr. in *The Panjab Past and Present*, 13/1 (Apr. 1979), 164–79.

[7] Webster, *The Nirankari Sikhs*, pp. 9–11, 31–2.

north-western portion of the Punjab. His successor, in contrast, was from the village of Bhaini Raian in Ludhiana District. Ram Singh, having succeeded Balak Singh, returned to his native village, and it was within Ludhiana District and adjacent areas that the new sect developed its principal following. Its adherents were from castes with a strong Khalsa affiliation (notably artisans and poorer Jats) and predictably the Namdhari sect assumed a self-conscious Khalsa identity termed *Sant Khālsā*. Like their Nirankari contemporaries, Balak Singh and Ram Singh believed that there had been a grievous corrupting of Sikh practice during the period of the Sikh kingdom. The two responses were, however, widely divergent. Whereas one sought a return to pristine Nanak-panthi principles, the other preached a restored and regenerated Khalsa.[8]

The stress which is characteristically laid on the emergence of these two movements can easily suggest that the authentic spirit of the Khalsa had indeed dwindled during the later years of political power. This, moreover, was to be a part of the message of the Singh Sabha movement, an interpretation of the Panth's history which endeavoured to explain the perceived decay of the mid-nineteenth century by blaming the insidious influence of political strength and material affluence.[9] Like so much of the Singh Sabha message, it is an interpretation which needs to be carefully scrutinized before it is accepted. For the Singh Sabha reformers it was an important interpretation, one which supplied a major link in the historiographical chain which they fashioned, and as such it contributed to the justification which they offered in defence of their proposed reforms. A critical scrutiny suggests that their emphasis on growing decadence was considerably exaggerated. Decadence may well have been a feature of the royal durbar after the death of Ranjit Singh. It was not necessarily a feature of Khalsa practice in general.[10]

A theory of mid-century decline and decadence was congenial to the Singh Sabha reformers because their insistence on reform was based on the belief that their own version of Khalsa doctrine derived from Guru Gobind Singh himself. Their view assumed that there had been a clear and detailed statement of the Khalsa duty during the lifetime of the tenth

---

[8] Gurmit Singh, *Sant Khalsa*, pp. 27–33.

[9] Harbans Singh, *The Heritage of the Sikhs*, p. 228.

[10] On the Singh Sabha in general (which, amongst much else, disputes the claim to decadence as grossly exaggerated), see Harjot Singh Oberoi, 'A World Reconstructed: Religion, Ritual and Community among the Sikhs, 1850–1909' (unpub. Ph.D. thesis, Australian National University, Canberra, 1987). For the discussion of alleged 'decadence', see esp. fos. 146–7.

Guru, and later practice which deviated from that statement represented ignorance or perversity.[11] The task of the reformer must thus be to purge excrescence and recover what had been lost.

As we have already seen, however, the Khalsa Rahit was in the process of evolution during the course of the eighteenth century and by modern standards it was still only partially formulated by the end of that century. The outward forms of the Khalsa tradition which emerged during the course of the eighteenth century seem to have undergone comparatively little change during the first half of the nineteenth. Gurdwaras evidently assumed a larger importance during the more settled conditions imposed by Sikh rule, but the kind of Khalsa Sikh whom Joseph Cunningham observed during the period 1838–46 seems very similar to those whom Malcolm and his predecessors had described at the turn of the century.

In describing the customs and 'distinctive usages of the Sikhs', Cunningham refers to the merging of castes, the Khalsa rite of initiation, 'devotion to steel' (swords in all cases and also bracelets in the case of those zealous soldiers, the Akalis), uncut hair, blue clothing, use of the name 'Singh', and a strict ban on smoking.[12] The *kachh* (which he describes as 'a kind of breeches' or, in the more modern style 'a sort of pantaloons') is, he observes, a garment of particular importance, clearly distinguishing Sikhs from Hindus.[13] The presence of the Guru was recognized in 'the *Granth* of Nanak' (that is, the Adi Granth) and in any gathering of five Sikhs.[14] Frequently one heard the exclamation 'Wah Guru', or perhaps the lengthened versions 'Wah! Guru ki Fat[e]h' and 'Wah! Guru ka Khalsa'.[15]

Cunningham also agrees with Malcolm in affirming that Sikhs should be regarded as 'different from other Indians', and that, in spite of obvious resemblances in language and everyday customs, this involves a clear distinction between Sikhs and Hindus.[16] He is, however, more emphatic than Malcolm in emphasizing the predominance of the Khalsa identity amongst Sikhs. Nanak-panthis are to be found scattered through the cities of India and there exist several Sikh sects, but 'the great development of the tenets of Guru Gobind has thrown other denominations into the shade'. Within the Punjab at least the Khalsa identity prevails amongst those who regard themselves as Sikhs.[17]

---

[11] Kanh Singh Nabha, *Gurmat sudhākar* (1st edn., Amritsar, 1901; rev. edn., Patiala, 1970), intro.

[12] J. D. Cunningham, *A History of the Sikhs* (1st edn., London, 1849; rev. edn., Oxford, 1918), 70–4, 110, 346–9.   [13] Ibid. 349.

[14] Ibid. 82.   [15] Ibid. 347.

[16] Ibid. 84–5.   [17] Ibid. 90 n.

This perception is strongly supported by the Sikhs' own literature. The gur-bilas tradition extends well into the nineteenth century and at least two of its prominent contributors produced their major work during the final decade of the Sikh kingdom. The celebrated works of Santokh Singh were composed during the first half of the nineteenth century and *Sūraj Prakāś* (the work which includes his Khalsa coverage) appeared in 1844. Three years earlier that most notable of all Khalsa dissertations had been completed. This was Ratan Singh Bhangu's *Prāchīn Panth Prakāś*, a work which vigorously affirms the distinctive nature of the Khalsa identity and the claim that this was the identity which Guru Gobind Singh intended his followers to adopt.[18]

The tradition is one which extends across the years of 'decadence' and into the period of Singh Sabha reform. Gian Singh's *Panth Prakāś* was issued in 1880, and the final instalment of his *Tavarīkh Gurū Khālsā* did not appear until 1919. By the time *Tavarīkh Gurū Khālsā* was completed, the Rahit had acquired its modern form and the works of Gian Singh can appropriately be regarded as examples of the unfolding pattern of Rahit observance. They can also be regarded as examples of the sustained predominance of the Khalsa identity, extending through from the early eighteenth century to the early twentieth century and onwards to the present day.[19]

The nineteenth-century rahit-nama tradition evidently communicates the same message, though in terms which are rather more difficult to decode. A serious problem persists because the rahit-namas which were current during the middle decades of the nineteenth century cannot yet be firmly located with regard to either time or place of composition. Until their contexts are identified and understood, all such texts must be used with great caution.

[18] In 1809 (s. 1866) Ratan Singh Bhangu, at Sir David Ochterlony's request, had provided Captain Murray in Ludhiana with information concerning the Khalsa. This he published in verse in 1841 (s. 1898) as *Panth Prakāś*, later known as *Prāchīn Panth Prakāś* to distinguish it from Gian Singh's work of the same name. Ratan Singh came from a distinguished Khalsa lineage, being the grandson of Matab Singh Bhangu who killed Massa Ranghar for desecrating Harimandir Sahib in 1740. Kahn Singh Nabha, *Guruśabad ratanākar mahān koś* (2nd rev. edn., Patiala, 1960), 594–5. Koer Singh's *Gur-bilās Pātaśāhī 10* and Sohan's *Gur-bilās Chhevīn Pātaśāhī* both claim to be eighteenth-century works. It has, however, been shown that both belong to the early nineteenth century. S. S. Hans, 'Gurbilas Patshahi 10 and Gurbilas Chhevin Patshahi as Sources for Early Nineteenth Century Punjab History', in Fauja Singh and A. C. Arora (ed.), *Maharaja Ranjit Singh: Politics, Society and Economy* (Patiala, 1984), 50–5. Id., 'Social Transformation and the Creative Imagination in Sikhism', in Sudhir Chandra (ed.), *Social Transformation and Creative Imagination* (New Delhi, 1984), pp. 104–6.

[19] McLeod (trans.), *Textual Sources for the Study of Sikhism*, pp. 12–13.

The fact that certain rahit-namas were in use during those middle decades can nevertheless be accepted as significant, and it seems likely that two of the major rahit-namas were actually composed during this period. These are the *Prem Sumārg* and the *Sau Sākhīān*.[20] Meanwhile (as Cunningham notes) the brief works attributed to Nand Lal and Prahilad Singh were in current circulation and were evidently accepted as authentic statements of the Rahit.[21] The Khalsa which is portrayed in these texts is not yet the Khalsa envisaged by the Singh Sabha reformers, but the line of development is clear and likewise the dominant features of the Khalsa identity as described by these rahit-namas.

If this should suggest that all was well with the Khalsa during the middle decades of the nineteenth century, the view is one which, looking back, the adherents of the reformist Singh Sabha would vigorously deny. It must be clearly understood that we do not speak here of the Singh Sabha as such, for the Singh Sabha was soon to be divided.[22] Those who dominated the founding of the Amritsar branch in 1873 were pre-dominantly conservative Sikhs (Sanatan Sikhs) and it is not these men who concern us at present. It is the reformers, more common in the Lahore society, who agreed in large measure with the British observers' comments on the manifold signs of Khalsa decay. They certainly did not accept the common British assumption that decay spelt imminent dissolution, but it did seem likely that such would eventually be the fate of the Panth if vigorous measures were not taken to resuscitate the Khalsa ideal and restore traditional loyalties.

To the Singh Sabha reformers (at least the more ardent of them) disloyalty and decay were evident at all levels of Sikh society. Even Maharaja Ranjit Singh had betrayed the pure faith in death, distributing the material treasures of the Khalsa to Brahmans in the evident hope that he would thereby earn eternal merit. The same Brahmans participated prominently in his funeral rites and at the actual cremation four of his wives, together with seven 'slave girls', committed suttee.[23] The Maharaja's death epitomized both the danger and its source. It marked a threatening reassertion of Hindu tradition, the very superstitions which

[20] See chap. 3, n. 17. McLeod, 'The Problem of the Panjabi *rahit-nāmās*', in S. N. Mukherjee (ed.), *India: History and Thought* (Calcutta, 1982), pp. 116–17. Mohan Singh, *An Introduction to Punjabi Literature* (Amritsar, 1954), 121–30, effusively praises the contribution of the *Prem Sumārg*, though with reference to an earlier period.

[21] Cunningham, *A History of the Sikhs*, pp. 372–6.

[22] Harjot Singh Oberoi, 'A World Reconstructed: Religion, Ritual and Community among the Sikhs, 1850–1909' (unpub. Ph.D. thesis, Australian National University, Canberra, 1987), fos. 202 ff. and esp. chap. 6.

[23] Khushwant Singh, *A History of the Sikhs*, i. 289–90.

the Gurus had so vigorously denounced. If further evidence of the danger should be required, one need do no more than visit a gurdwara and observe the 'Hinduized' ritual practised therein. Even the precincts of the Golden Temple itself were disfigured by the presence of Hindu idols.[24] How, in such circumstances, could one deny the urgent compelling need for drastic reform?

Another 'Hindu' practice which conspicuously disfigured the nineteenth-century Panth was the observance of caste, particularly in terms of the discrimination applied to outcastes. To the Singh Sabha reformers the intention of the Gurus with regard to caste was crystal clear. The Gurus had denounced it in word and deed, conferring on their followers a scripture which incorporated the message and customs which gave it practical expression. How else could one construe the custom of sangat and pangat, the mingling of all in the langar, or the common water (*amrit*) of the initiation ceremony? Now, however, Sikhs were marrying strictly according to caste, and, following caste prescriptions, they ate in the manner of Hindus. Outcastes were prohibited from entering many gurdwaras and the sacred karah prasad was preserved from their contamination.[25]

The beliefs and customs of the Panth's élite supplied numerous examples of decadence and dire decay. Village life provided many more. In the villages of the Punjab it was often impossible to distinguish a Sikh from a Hindu and this was not merely because the outward symbols of the Khalsa were so indifferently observed. Frequently it was because the villager was quite unaware of the essential difference between a Hindu and a Sikh, easily moving from one identity to another and promis-cuously combining elements from both. Indeed, the villager who was meant to be a Sikh might well adopt beliefs and practices which manifestly derived from Muslim sources. Seeking favours at the tombs of Muslim pirs was merely one such example. How could people who worshipped Gugga Pir or Sakhi Sarwar be regarded as loyal Sikhs of the Khalsa?[26] How could men who so brazenly cut their hair or smoked the hookah be accepted as devout servants of the Guru.

The facts were plain for all to see. The solution was also obvious, at least for those who accepted Singh Sabha analysis of a reformist persuasion. The Panth must be purged of false beliefs and superstitions,

[24] Harbans Singh, 'Origin of the Singh Sabha', in Harbans Singh and N. Gerald Barrier (eds.), *Punjab Past and Present: Essays in Honour of Dr Ganda Singh* (Patiala, 1976), 274.

[25] Teja Singh, *Essays in Sikhism* (Lahore, 1944), 133.

[26] Harjot Singh Oberoi, 'The Worship of Pir Sakhi Sarvar: Illness, Healing and Popular Culture in the Punjab', *Studies in History* NS 3/1 (1987), 50–3.

both Hindu or Muslim. Sikhs must be summoned to a genuine reaffirmation of their Khalsa loyalty.

One other element deserves to be noted before we survey the various interpretations of the Singh Sabha movement. This concerns the contribution of the Indian Army. The British had been impressed by the strength of the opposition which they encountered during the two Anglo-Sikh wars and, although they were initially suspicious of their defeated enemies, their attitude towards the Sikhs changed significantly as a result of the assistance which they received from Sikh princes during the Mutiny. Sikhs were easily accommodated within the British theory of the martial races of India and Sikh enlistment increased steeply. For the British, however, martial Sikhs meant Khalsa Sikhs, and all who were inducted into the Indian Army as Sikhs were required to maintain the external insignia of the Khalsa.[27] This policy and its effective enforcement provide a significant element in the debate concerning Sikh identity during the crucial half-century from 1875 to 1925. As we shall see, the intention of the British policy and more particularly its practical effect have been variously interpreted.

The first Singh Sabha, as we have already noted, was formed in 1873. Four Sikh students attending the Mission School in Amritsar had announced their intention of taking Christian baptism and this event was evidently the reason for a meeting convened in the city by a group of prominent Sikhs. The first meeting was followed by others and from these discussions there emerged the decision to found a society called the Singh Sabha. Titled gentry, affluent landowners, and noted scholars were conspicuous amongst its founders, and the objectives which they framed for their new association gave expression to their distinctive ideals. Particular emphasis was laid on the promotion of periodicals and other appropriate literature, the assumption being that those who needed to be influenced would be accessible through the printed word. British officers were invited to associate with the Sabha and matters relating to government were expressly excluded from its range of interests.[28] The first

---

[27] Khushwant Singh, *A History of the Sikhs*, ii (Princeton, 1966), 113. See also R. W. Falcon, *Handbook on the Sikhs for the Use of Regimental Officers* (Allahabad, 1896); and A. H. Bingley, *Sikhs* (Simla, 1899), esp. chap. v.

[28] Rajiv A. Kapur, *Sikh Separatism: The Politics of Faith* (London, 1986), 16–17. For excellent summaries of the Singh Sabha, see the recent works of N. Gerald Barrier: 'The Roots of Modern Sikhism', in *Aspects of Modern Sikhism* (Michigan Papers on Sikh Studies, No. 1; 1985), 1–12; 'Sikh Politics in British Punjab Prior to the Gurdwara Reform Movement', in J. D. O'Connell *et al.* (eds.), *Sikh History and Religion in the Twentieth Century* (Toronto, 1988), 159–90; 'The Singh Sabhas and the Evolution of Modern Sikhism, 1875–1925', in Robert Baird (ed.), *Religious Movements in Modern India* (New

Singh Sabha was an élite organization, very similar to the urban associations which were emerging in other parts of India but specifically concerned with issues affecting the Sikh Panth.

Although the Singh Sabha movement never lost its élite texture, the Amritsar originators soon found themselves challenged by more strident exponents of the newly fledged ideal. In 1879 a second Singh Sabha was founded in Lahore and, although the two societies devised similar charters, the Lahore group soon proved to be much the more aggressive. Whereas the Amritsar organization was dominated by princely and landed interests, the Singh Sabha in Lahore attracted intellectuals with a more radical approach to the Panth's problems. Prominent amongst them was Giani Dit Singh, an outcaste Sikh who vigorously promoted social reform and a return to the casteless ideal of the Khalsa. Most radical of all was the small but embarrassingly noisy Singh Sabha of Bhasaur, led by Teja Singh Overseer.[29]

Each of these Singh Sabhas (particularly Amritsar and Lahore) attracted satellites as new sabhas were formed in various towns and villages. One feature which, in a general sense, distinguished the principal constellations was the contrast in their respective attitudes towards Khalsa exclusiveness. Amritsar, influenced by the weighty presence of Baba Khem Singh Bedi, tended strongly to support the claims of Sahaj-dhari Sikhs to an honoured place within the Panth. Bhasaur, at the other extreme, was militantly fundamentalist. The Lahore group also adopted a strict line, but with a somewhat sweeter reason and a more restrained idiom. Eventually its view came to be accepted as orthodox. The Khalsa tradition was to be regarded as standard. Sahaj-dharis were to be accepted only as 'slow-adopters', aspiring to the full status of the baptized Amrit-dhari Sikh but not yet ready to take formal initiation.[30]

Those who represented the reformist sector of the Singh Sabha movement came to be known as the Tat Khalsa (the 'True Khalsa' or the 'Pure Khalsa'). Opposing them, and increasingly disadvantaged by the strength of Tat Khalsa ideals and determination, were the conservatives of the so-called Sanatan Khalsa. By the turn of the century the exponents of Tat Khalsa theory had asserted an effective claim to interpret the nature of tradition and to enunciate the approved pattern of Sikh

Delhi, forthcoming); 'The Sikhs and Punjab Politics, 1882–1922', in Paul Wallace and Surendra Chopra (ed.), *Political Dynamics of the Punjab* (Amritsar, 1981; 2nd edn., forthcoming); etc.

[29] N. Gerald Barrier, *The Sikhs and their Literature* (Delhi, 1970), pp. xxvi–xxvii.

[30] Teja Singh, *Essays in Sikhism*, p. 117. N. Gerald Barrier, 'The Singh Sabhas and the Evolution of Modern Sikhism, 1875–1925'.

behaviour. When we speak of the Singh Sabha movement, we normally refer to its Tat Khalsa sector. When we describe the historiography, doctrinal formulations, and social policy of the Singh Sabha, we invariably do so.[31]

Prominent amongst the Tat Khalsa reformers were scholars such as Bhai Kahn Singh of Nabha and the prolifically versatile writer Bhai Vir Singh. Closely associated with them was the Englishman M. A. Macauliffe.[32] Together with others who shared the same attitudes and concerns, these authors were responsible for moulding and recording a version of the Sikh tradition which remains dominant in intellectual circles to the present day. It is important to remember that, when we read literature dealing with the Sikh tradition, we are usually reading perceptions which have been refracted through a Tat Khalsa lens. The reminder is essential if we are to achieve genuine detachment in any analysis of Sikh history, doctrine, or behaviour. Repeatedly we must draw attention to the impressive success achieved by scholars and writers associated with the Singh Sabha movement, for only thus can we hope to disengage our own interpretations from their continuing influence.

These men were largely responsible for the first of the interpretations which we must note in connection with the Singh Sabha. Their understanding of the Sikh tradition in general and the role of the Singh Sabha in particular can be summarized as follows.

Although Guru Nanak was born a Hindu, he separated his followers from Hindu society by requiring them to renounce caste. This intention

[31] A detailed analysis of the origin, nature, and spread of Tat Khalsa beliefs is given by Harjot Singh Oberoi, 'A World Reconstructed', chaps. 6–7. The thesis brings out very clearly the critical differences between the two principal groups within the Singh Sabha. The conclusion on fo. 307 deserves to be noted. See also id., 'From Ritual to Counter-ritual: Rethinking the Hindu-Sikh Question, 1884–1915', in J. D. O'Connell *et al.* (eds.), *Sikh History and Religion in the Twentieth Century*, pp. 136–58. The distinction is also clearly noted by N. Gerald Barrier in 'The Singh Sabhas and the Evolution of Modern Sikhism, 1875–1925'. In his 'The Sikhs and Punjab Politics, 1882–1922' it is identified as the 'Lahore or Tat Khalsa . . . message'. The other works of Harjot Singh Oberoi also deserve to be noted, in particular his 'Bhais, Babas and Gyanis: Traditional Intellectuals in Nineteenth Century Punjab', *Studies in History*, 2/2 (1980), 33–62 (a study of the Amritsar Singh Sabha leadership); and 'A Historical and Bibliographical Reconstruction of the Singh Sabha in Nineteenth Century Punjab', *Journal of Sikh Studies*, 10/3 (Aug. 1983), 108–30. The second of these refers to the principal differences distinguishing Sanatan and Tat Khalsa Sikhs on pp. 116–17.

[32] Sukhjit Kaur, *Bhāī Kāhn Siṅgh Nābhā te unhāṅ diāṅ rachanāvāṅ* (Patiala, n.d.). Harbans Singh, *Bhai Vir Singh* (New Delhi, 1972), Id., 'English Translation of the Sikh Scripture: An Arduous Mission of a Punjab Civilian', in K. S. Bedi and S. S. Bal (eds.), *Essays on History, Literature, Art and Culture Presented to Dr M. S. Randhawa* (New Delhi, 1970), 139–44.

was expressly stated by Guru Arjan in the words 'We are neither Hindu nor Muslim',[33] and definitively confirmed by Guru Gobind Singh with the founding of the Khalsa. By establishing the Khalsa the tenth Guru bestowed on his followers a particular insignia (the Five Ks) and required them to observe a distinctive way of life. Admission to the recreated Panth was by initiation (the baptismal ceremony of *amrit sanskār*). All loyal followers of the Guru were expected to accept initiation and in so doing they were required to acknowledge the obligations of the Rahit.

The decades which followed the inauguration of the Khalsa brought a time of trial. Some faced the cruelty and fierce persecution with courage and determined loyalty, embracing martyrdom rather than betray their faith. Others, weaker in commitment, fell by the wayside. Eventually victory went to the brave and with the nineteenth century there came the period of triumph under Maharaja Ranjit Singh. The Khalsa ruled and with Ranjit Singh as leader it advanced to even greater glories.

Yet power can corrupt even the Khalsa. Political success and material affluence proved to be compelling temptations and many of the Khalsa were seduced by them. Hindu customs progressively reasserted their hold within the Panth, and, following the British annexation of the Punjab, this alarming tendency reached dangerous proportions. The British policy of insisting on Khalsa observances within the Indian Army helped to sustain the traditional loyalty, but because it affected such a small segment of the total Sikh population it could not provide a sufficient answer to the rapidly growing threat of disintegration.

It was to meet this challenge that the Singh Sabha movement was initiated, or at least so the Tat Khalsa believed. The message which it proclaimed was a simple one, easily comprehended and easily applied. Recognize that the Guru created a separate Panth, free from superstition and true to the doctrine of the divine Name. Recognize that all who seek membership in the Guru's Panth must accept the Guru's Rahit and that each must accordingly become a Sikh of the Khalsa. Recognize that *ham hindū nahīn*, we are not Hindus.[34] A Sanatan Sikh might demur, but for the Tat Khalsa it was obvious.

This interpretation has been vigorously contested by many who chose to identify as Sahaj-dhari Sikhs and by many more Punjabi Hindus who

---

[33] Guru Arjan, *Bhairau* 3, Adi Granth p. 1136. See chap. 2, n. 27.

[34] Two short works by Teja Singh summarize this point of view. See *Sikhism: Its Ideals and Institutions* (rev. edn., Bombay, 1951) and *Essays in Sikhism*. The title of a booklet by Kahn Singh Nabha first issued in 1899, *Ham Hindū nahīn*, was perhaps the most famous of all Singh Sabha publications.

laid no claims to a formal affiliation with the Panth. According to this second interpretation, Guru Nanak was a Hindu who remained a Hindu and who intended that his followers should likewise retain their traditional identities. There have been innumerable panths within the larger Hindu tradition and the panth of Guru Nanak is no different from the others in terms of its relationship to Hindu society. One may choose to follow the *nām simaraṇ* discipline taught by Nanak, but one does not thereby cease to be a Hindu (nor indeed a Muslim if that should be the inherited identity).

In establishing the Khalsa the tenth Guru certainly introduced a new element of great significance, but the relationship of the Sikh Panth to Hindu society remained unchanged. The Khalsa is a voluntary society within the Sikh Panth, formed to protect Hindus from Mughal aggression. Those who call themselves Sikhs have ever since had the choice of joining this strictly regulated society or of maintaining the kind of Nanak-panthi allegiance which was appropriate for all Sikhs prior to 1699. All remain Hindus, whether baptized Amrit-dhari or shaven Sahaj-dhari. All revere the Gurus and all who are devout will regularly visit a gurdwara for *darśan* of Guru Granth Sahib. Sikhs continue to observe caste, and Sikh marries Hindu in precisely the same way that Hindus traditionally intermarry. Some families observe the custom of having the eldest son initiated as an Amrit-dhari Sikh while all other members retain the identity of conventional Hindus.[35]

Some add that the real villains were the British. It was the British (so this extended version maintains) who taught the Sikhs to see themselves as distinct from other Indians and eventually to perceive the Panth as a separate 'nation'. This they achieved partly through their army practice, requiring all Sikh recruits to observe the Khalsa symbols and encouraging the Sikhs to see themselves as a 'martial race'. In part it was also achieved by means of an education which taught its pupils to think in Western terms. These involve clear distinctions whereas Indian tradition encourages the eirenic blurring of division and resolutely refuses to erect unbreachable barriers. Sikhs were also taught to see themselves as monotheists and to spurn the 'idolatry' of Hindus. Macauliffe was a notorious offender, ably assisted by Sikhs who had been trained to think

---

[35] Dharam Pal Ashta, 'Sikhism as an Off-shoot of Traditional Hinduism and as a Response to the Challenge of Islam' in *Sikhism and Indian Society* (Transactions of the Indian Institute of Advanced Study, vol. 4; Simla, 1967), 230–46. Gokul Chand Narang, *Transformation of Sikhism* (1st edn., Lahore, 1914; rev. edn., Lahore, 1946), app. ii–iii, pp. 346–69. Kapur, *Sikh Separatism*, p. 5.

in a Western mode. Christian missionaries added their enthusiastic support to the campaign.[36]

These two interpretations (the 'Sikh' and the 'Hindu') represent extreme views. In theoretical terms it is possible to formulate intermediate versions of Sikh identity. It is, for example, possible to argue that the Sahaj-dhari or Nanak-panthi identity is exclusively Sikh and that those who adopt it are no more Hindu than Sikhs of the Khalsa. In practice, however, one seldom hears such claims. Punjabis who believe that identities should be precisely formulated normally adopt one or other of the two interpretations summarized above. The debate has followed these lines throughout the present century, the intensity rising or falling as circumstances create divisive issues within Punjabi society or encourage a general sense of social satisfaction. Needless to say, it has risen sharply since the assault on the Golden Temple complex in June 1984. One seldom hears mention of Sahaj-dharis in the late 1980s, although that does not necessarily mean that the species is endangered or extinct.

Although the two interpretations are diametrically opposed, both suffer from the same basic flaw. Both are strictly intellectual formulations and both manipulate the historical past in order to defend contemporary perceptions. There is nothing unusual about such a procedure. It is perfectly normal, as all students of history should surely know. Accepting it as normal does not mean, however, that we must accept the procedure as sound historical analysis. Against it must be set two major objections, each of them affirming that these traditional interpretations are much too simple to be acceptable.

The first objection is implicit in our earlier treatment of the development of the Khalsa over a period of two eventful centuries. Though the linkage be both fundamental and obvious, the Khalsa which confronts us in the twentieth century is not the Khalsa of the early eighteenth century. The Singh Sabha interpretation distorts this reality by claiming that they are indeed identical in terms of their essential features, differing only because certain features of the tradition have been corrupted. This ignores the never-ending sequence of responses which any religious group must necessarily make to changing circumstances. Only the moribund escape this obligation.

The same general criticism applies to those who affirm the 'Hindu' interpretation. Changing circumstances mean changing attitudes and

[36] Sita Ram Goel, intro. to Ram Swarup, *Hindu–Sikh Relationship* (New Delhi, 1985), 7–9. Ram Swarup, ibid. 12–15.

changing identities. Whatever the original intention of Guru Nanak may have been, there can be no doubt about either the transforming influence of later experience or the attitude which has long been dominant within the Panth. Any attempt to persuade Khalsa Sikhs that they are Hindus is futile. Those Sikhs who are concerned with the defining of identities know that they are not Hindus and the rest of us must accept that assertion as a fact.

The second objection to both interpretations is that most people (Sikhs included) are not much bothered with identity differences, except perhaps in times of crisis. We must ever be aware that intellectual formulations are typically the concern of those who, by virtue of education, occupation, or family tradition, are encouraged to pursue such objectives. Much of the 'Who is a Sikh?' debate is, in fact, conducted within that area of Punjabi society which is occupied by the Khatri, Arora, and Ahluwalia castes, and it should come as no surprise to discover that such conventions as the baptizing of elder sons should be largely restricted to families from these castes. Jat society has fewer problems of definition precisely because it provides much less encouragement to debate. A Jat Sikh knows that he is a Sikh and there, for most, the matter ends.

The true nature of the problem can be easily understood by attempting to locate both Amrit-dhari and Kes-dhari Sikhs within a single consistent theory of Khalsa identity. For most it is not a problem because in normal circumstances few would question a Kes-dhari's claim to be accepted as a Sikh. It is only when the intellectual formulation assumes major importance that the issue becomes even remotely significant, and such occasions are rare. Even the so-called 'fundamentalist', ardent in advocating *amrit sanskār*, will normally accept a non-smoking Kes-dhari as a Sikh. If, however, one insists upon strict intellectual consistency, two options quickly emerge. Either one deregisters all but the diligent Amrit-dhari, or alternatively one faces endless confusion.

Discussions of this kind involve endless debate with no prospect of agreement. If we are to understand the role of the Singh Sabha and the nature of Sikh identity at the turn of the century, history must be used much more critically and the analysis thus produced will have to be rather more intricate. Any such analysis must certainly recognize the continuity which extends from the earliest days of the Nanak-panth to the end of the nineteenth century and beyond. By itself, however, this is insufficient. The force of intervening circumstances must also be recognized and the history of the Panth, like all history, must be seen as an

endlessly evolving pattern. This may be regarded as the most elementary
of historical truisms. The point nevertheless needs to be grasped if our
discussion of Sikh identity is to proceed on rational lines.

A recent contribution which recognizes this need is Richard Fox's
Lions of the Punjab.[37] Fox actually concentrates his attention on the
Akali movement and on what he calls the 'Third Sikh War' of 1920–5
(usually known as the Gurdwara Reform Movement).[38] Much of his
basic analysis nevertheless concerns the Singh Sabha period and the
identity which developed under its auspices. The relevant portion of his
argument may be summarized as follows.

The British, having conquered the Punjab, set about integrating it into
the capitalist world economy. In so doing they successively pursued two
conflicting policies. Whereas the earlier policy favoured a continuation of
traditional agrarian production, the later version involved large-scale
state investment in canal irrigation. The former policy encouraged the
development of a rural class of petty commodity producers in central
Punjab and also provided an opportunity for trading castes to form a
lower-middle class.[39] The latter were initially attracted to the Arya Samaj
(the radical Hindu society which was particularly strong in the Punjab),
but, when a militant section of the Samaj attacked Sikh traditions, those
who subscribed to those traditions went their separate way.[40]

The path which they elected to follow was one which had already been
demarcated and defined by the British. The British had inherited a
Punjab in which the term 'Sikh' carried no precise or agreed meaning. It
covered a varied range of differing identities, no one of them accepted as
standard or orthodox.[41] The British selected one of the available
identities (the Khalsa identity) and insisted that its army recruits should
thereafter observe routine Khalsa standards.[42] This identity was also
assumed by those members of the trading castes who sought economic
and educational advantage on the basis of their claim to be Sikhs.[43] They
in turn communicated it to the petty commodity producers of central
Punjab, already well prepared for its adoption by instruction received in
the Indian Army.[44]

---

[37] Richard G. Fox, *Lions of the Punjab: Culture in the Making* (Berkeley and Los
Angeles, 1985).

[38] The term 'Third Sikh War' was introduced by the Akali activist Sardul Singh
Caveeshar, *The Sikh Studies* (Lahore, 1937), 191 ff.

[39] Fox, *Lions of the Punjab*, chaps. 2–4 *passim*.   [40] Ibid. 166–8.

[41] Ibid. 108–16.   [42] Ibid., chap. 8 and p. 178.

[43] Ibid. 168–71.

[44] Ibid. 80, 171–9.

During the early years of the twentieth century both the urban lower-middle class and the petty commodity producers of the villages experienced increasing economic pressure as a result of the investment policies more recently introduced by the British.[45] In addition to this shift in economic policy the British were also endeavouring to assert a more effective dominance over the Sikhs by controlling their gurdwaras.[46] By the time serious economic crisis developed after the First World War those most affected by it had been taught to regard themselves as Khalsa Sikhs and to perceive the incumbent owners of the gurdwaras (the mahants) as traitors to the Khalsa cause. A struggle which developed for economic reasons thus assumed the guise of a religious campaign.

Fox insists that his analysis should not be construed as simply a materialist explanation. Cultural factors were also involved. He maintains, however, that the latter are quite inadequate as an explanation for the developments which occurred during the early decades of the twentieth century. A basic feature of his argument is that

those who labeled themselves 'Sikh' in the nineteenth century embraced no single cultural meaning, religious identity, or social practice; rather, an amalgam of what later reformers made into separate Hindu and Sikh cultural principles prevailed. Therefore, long-standing, widely shared, and consistent Sikh cultural principles cannot explain why the Third Sikh War was fought on the basis of Singh identity and over Sikh institutions. *In fact, no such tradition existed*.[47]

In thus isolating the identity issue we do some violence to the total argument which Fox develops. It is, however, fundamental to his theory as a whole as to our own present concerns, and it deserves to be scrutinized in isolation. In so doing we should acknowledge the truth of his claim that the nineteenth-century Panth incorporated a variety of identities.[48] As he presents it, however, the claim amounts to a serious exaggeration. To imply that no dominant tradition existed is to ignore the clear evidence of earlier periods. Although the Khalsa was not the sole claimant to the title of Sikh, it was by far the strongest and it carried into the British period conventions which enable us to recognize a clear connection between the Khalsa of the eighteenth century and that of the twentieth. The suggestion that the 'Singh identity' was selected by the British and then appropriated by a particular caste group for its own class

[45] Ibid. 76–8.
[46] Ibid. 158–9.
[47] Ibid. 106 (my italics). For a similar claim, see ibid. 116. Fox summarizes his argument on pp. 11–13 and 207–11.
[48] See also Harjot Singh Oberoi, 'A World Reconstructed', fos. 147–60.

purposes is unacceptable. As a theory it is no more valid than the claim that the Khalsa identity was invented by radical members of the Singh Sabha.

Such theories are nevertheless useful in that they stress the existence of alternate identities and the extent to which the Khalsa version acquired coherence during the Singh Sabha period. Fox also carries us closer to an acceptable analysis by emphasizing the role of the British. Although the emphasis which he lays on their economic and military policies may be altogether excessive, both features should certainly be incorporated in any such analysis. With them must come several other elements. As in other parts of India, the British presence in the Punjab amounted to much more than economic exploitation and a recruiting agency. Their economic influence was indeed significant, but we distort its results if we neglect the total range of their influence. There is a much larger context to be considered, and it is only within that larger context that the consequences of their presence can be appreciated.

The contribution of the British to Punjabi society involved economic policies, patterns of administration, a new technology, a fresh approach to education, and entry for Christian missionaries. Needless to say these elements did not operate in isolation, each exerting a distinct and separate influence on different areas of Punjabi society. Instead they meshed together, producing a web of influences which variously affected all Punjabis. Inherited status combined with new-found affluence might provide access to an education which supplied ideas subsequently propagated by means of printing presses. Economy, administration, education, and technology could combine to exert new pressures on Punjabi society and thus induce fundamental changes in that society.[49]

The emergence of the Singh Sabha movement provides a particularly important example of precisely this pattern. Most of the men who met in Amritsar or Lahore to form the first Singh Sabhas in 1873 and 1879 were from Sikh élites, those which had buttressed traditional status with British preferment. They were reacting to a perceived attack on their inherited traditions, and these traditions were to be defended in whatever ways might seem appropriate. The traditions derived from their pre-British past, reflecting the earlier acceptance of a dominant Khalsa with a Nanak-panthi appendage. The chosen methods of defence expressed educational influences and the available technology, a pattern which became increasingly evident as the movement progressed.

---

[49] Ibid., fos. 186–201.

The pattern which developed clearly reflected modes of thinking and ideals which the more influential of the Tat Khalsa reformers had acquired from their education and from the Western literature to which they were increasingly exposed. Prompted by these influences, they began to produce definitions and to shape systems which were congenial to a Western understanding. In so doing, however, they remained loyal to the inherited tradition. It was a Sikh tradition, and specifically a Khalsa tradition, which they developed and glossed. To suggest that they developed a new tradition is false. Equally it is false to claim that their treatment of it can be described as a simple purging of alien excrescence or the restoration of a corrupted original. The Khalsa of the Singh Sabha reformers was both old and new.

The Khalsa ideal which thus emerged from the Singh Sabha period was distinguished by a new consistency and a new clarity of definition. Earlier features which no longer seemed acceptable were abandoned or drastically modified, one notable result being a conscious shift away from the Panth's traditional hostility towards Muslims. Various practices were vigorously debated, the quest for distinctive rituals was initiated, and attempts were made to produce acceptable statements of the Rahit. An appropriate version of the Panth's history was formulated, a powerful stress was laid on the doctrine of the Guru Granth, and Sikhs were exhorted to observe conventions which would proclaim their separate Khalsa identity. Prominent amongst these conventions was observance of the Five Ks. A fierce debate developed with Arya Samaj apologists and insistent stress was laid on the claim that Sikhs could never be regarded as Hindus.

Throughout this process of study and debate we can observe the pressure of contemporary attitudes operating on the desire to protect traditional loyalties. Many Sikhs still rejected the claim that they were distinct from Hindu society, but within the Singh Sabha this Sanatan view was strongly opposed by the increasingly dominant Tat Khalsa.[50] The campaign to place a specifically Sikh wedding ritual on the statute books illustrates the nature of the general controversy and the kind of result which the reformers were seeking.

The marriage order which they so vigorously proposed was Anand Karaj, a rite which featured four circuits of the Adi Granth by the groom and his bride. Sikhs had earlier conducted marriages with a fire ceremony. Whereas this looked suspiciously like Hindu ritual, the Anand

---

[50] Ibid., fos. 278 ff.

ceremony was plainly Sikh and it was claimed that the rite represented early Sikh practice. Although this latter claim must be questioned, there can be no doubting the Sikh content of the ritual nor the ordered dignity which it presents. It well expressed the Tat Khalsa ideal and a vigorous campaign preceded the passing of the Anand Marriage Act in 1909. Within a comparatively short time Anand Karaj had become the standard form for Sikh marriages, a testimony to the determination of the reformers and to the influence which they had acquired.[51]

The successes achieved by the Tat Khalsa intellectuals and their supporters did not mean that the battle for an approved identity had been won by the time the Singh Sabha movement began to wane in the early twentieth century. Neither the passion of Giani Dit Singh nor the immensely versatile pen of Bhai Vir Singh could instantly dispatch attitudes which had persisted through much of the Panth's history. In particular there remained the problem of the Sahaj-dharis. Were they also to be regarded as Sikhs or was the Khalsa identity to be the only acceptable one? If the Sahaj-dharis were to be acknowledged as Sikhs, should their characteristic sense of a dual identity be conceded? Was it possible to live with their claim that they were both Hindu and Sikh?

The Tat Khalsa reformers were not the only people interested in the problem. The British had been responsible for much of the creative ferment which produced the Singh Sabha movement. They were now being forced to look closely at the question of who could legally be regarded as a Sikh.

[51] Harjot S. Oberoi, 'From Ritual to Counter-ritual: Rethinking the Hindu–Sikh Question, 1884–1915', pp. 150–53. The Nirankari Sikhs maintain that the Tat Khalsa borrowed the Anand ceremony from them. Webster, *The Nirankari Sikhs*, pp. 16–18. See R. S. Talwar, 'Anand Marriage Act', *The Panjab Past and Present*, 2/2 (Oct. 1968), 400–10.

Definition by Legislation

DURING its early years the Singh Sabha spoke in uncertain tones. Some individuals were convinced that the essence of the Panth was the casteless Khalsa and that Sikhs must be persuaded to see themselves as distinct from Hindu society. Others were much less certain that loyalty to their inherited tradition demanded such radical consistency. For the more conservative supporter of the Singh Sabha movement, attacks on caste observance, shared rituals, and multiple Sikh identities could go too far. These were routine aspects of the life which he knew, and, although reforms were evidently needed, the demands of the enthusiasts were altogether excessive.

Thus did Sanatan Sikhs regard the ideology of the Tat Khalsa, and it was only gradually that Tat Khalsa views gained ascendancy amongst the intellectual leaders of the Panth. Many of those who could be regarded as radical were not initially impressed by claims that Sikhs were so very different from Hindus. This was clearly indicated by the strong support which the Arya Samaj received from many Sikhs in its early days. For some the principal reason may have been the strength of the Arya Samaj amongst members of the Khatri and Arora trading castes, a constituency which also supplied many prominent members of the Panth. For others it was evidently the Arya Samaj rejection of idol worship and its apparent willingness to accept outcastes.[1] Whatever the reason, a close association with the Arya Samaj was unlikely to strengthen notions of an absolute distinction between Sikhs and Hindus.

Eventually the Tat Khalsa radicals did secure dominance within the Singh Sabha, at least with regard to doctrinal formulations and literary output. The early alliance with the Arya Samaj was soon abandoned by all but a handful of Sikhs, partly because of attacks on Sikh traditions by a sector of its adherents and partly because the two movements found themselves competing for outcaste support.[2] The Singh Sabha of

---

[1] Kenneth W. Jones, *Arya Dharm: Hindu Consciousness in 19th-century Punjab* (New Delhi, 1976), 2–6, 135–6.

[2] Ibid. 137–9. N. Gerald Barrier, *The Sikhs and their Literature* (Delhi, 1970), pp. xxxiv–xxxvii.

Amritsar continued to reflect the Sanatan conservatism of many of its early supporters, but increasingly the philosophical initiative passed to the more radical men who dominated the Lahore group.[3]

Although such prominent activists as Dit Singh and Gurmukh Singh were associated with the Lahore Singh Sabha, this should not suggest a simple distinction between Amritsar conservatives and Lahore radicals.[4] Both Singh Sabhas (with their respective satellites) had memberships spanning a range of attitudes and in neither group could one expect to find extreme opinions. Those whom we regard as radicals were actually men of very moderate views. Their strength, moreover, was the strength of ideas and effective communication rather than that of direct political influence. When the various Singh Sabhas united to form the Chief Khalsa Diwan in 1902, the leadership of the joint body was largely dominated by relatively conservative landowners such as Sundar Singh Majithia.[5]

For their own reasons these conservative leaders also supported many of the projects which served to advance the progressive cause. Khalsa College in Amritsar, founded with government assistance in 1892,[6] may have expressed the educational hopes of the radicals but that was not its sole function. It also reflected the status concerns of the Singh Sabha's more conservative supporters and their influence over its fortunes remained considerable.

In terms of debate and publications, however, the more conspicuous and influential contribution came from those who were eventually to be styled the Tat Khalsa. Exponents of the Tat Khalsa ideal promoted reform through education, journalism, and preaching. Although Khalsa College was certainly the most notable of the new educational institutions, it was by no means the only one. Literacy amongst Sikhs increased significantly during the Singh Sabha period and by 1921 it was approaching 10 per cent of all Sikh males.[7] For the educated élite there were newspapers, pamphlets, and books in English, Punjabi, and Urdu. For others the approach was through itinerant preaching and popular assemblies.[8]

[3] Barrier, *The Sikhs and their Literature*, pp. xxxii–xxxiii.

[4] Harbans Singh, *The Heritage of the Sikhs* (rev. 2nd edn., New Delhi, 1983), 252.

[5] Rajiv A. Kapur, *Sikh Separatism: The Politics of Faith* (London, 1986), 18. Khushwant Singh, *A History of the Sikhs*, ii (Princeton, 1966), 145.

[6] Harbans Singh, *The Heritage of the Sikhs*, pp. 245–8.

[7] Kapur, *Sikh Separatism*, pp. 40–1.

[8] N. Gerald Barrier, 'The Sikhs and Punjab Politics, 1882–1922', in Paul Wallace and Surendra Chopra (eds.), *Political Dynamics of the Punjab* (Amritsar, 1981; 2nd edn., forthcoming).

The key issue in this campaign was the nature of Sikh identity and during its course some ardent controversies were generated. One which greatly intensified the debate occurred with the death of the wealthy Dyal Singh Majithia in 1898. In his will Dyal Singh Majithia left his substantial fortune to a trust bearing his name. This was contested by his widow on the grounds that the bequest had been made in accordance with the Hindu law of inheritance and that, because her husband was a Sikh, the bequest was void. This claim required the Punjab High Court to determine whether or not Sikhs should be regarded as Hindus, a proposition which it eventually affirmed. In the meantime many others had joined in the fray. Two pamphlets appeared bearing the title *Sikh Hindū hain* ('Sikhs are Hindus'), both of them by Sikh authors. The contrary view was expressed in Kahn Singh Nabha's celebrated *Ham Hindū nahīn* ('We are not Hindus').[9]

Kahn Singh was also responsible for one of the several attempts made during this period to produce a coherent statement of the Rahit. In 1901 he published in Punjabi his *Guramat Sudhākar*, a compendium of works relating to the life and mission of Guru Gobind Singh.[10] Such a collection would obviously be expected to include material relating to the Rahit, but here Kahn Singh encountered a problem. Although there was much in the extant rahit-nama texts which met with his approval, there were also items which an enlightened Khalsa Sikh of the Singh Sabha period could scarcely be expected to accept. The solution which he adopted faithfully reflects the Singh Sabha approach to tradition, an approach which still commands substantial popularity today.[11]

The collection of rahit-nama extracts which appears in *Guramat Sudhākar* is no mere abridgement, nor is it a strictly representative selection from their material. It is a selection which mirrors the conviction of men such as Kahn Singh that the extant rahit-namas presented modified or corrupt versions of the tenth Guru's original Rahit. Whether by reason of ignorance or malice, they had acquired spurious items and some of them had discarded injunctions which the Guru must surely have uttered. If the harmful or misleading supplements were to be purged and authentic injunctions retained, a purer statement of the Rahit would emerge.

[9] Kapur, *Sikh Separatism*, p. 19.
[10] Wazir-i-Hind Press, Amritsar. The book had already been issued in 1898 in Hindi. A revised edition of *Guramat Sudhākar* is available published by the Languages Department, Patiala, 1970.
[11] Ibid., *Bhūmikā*, 1970 edn., pp. u–ch.

This procedure eliminated many of the problems raised by the earlier rahit-namas without delivering a statement which would fully and accurately match Tat Khalsa ideals. The quest for an agreed rahit-nama continued and it remained unresolved throughout the Singh Sabha period. Much of the characteristic Singh Sabha understanding was incorporated in a manual of appropriate rituals issued by the Chief Khalsa Diwan in 1915 under the title *Guramat Prakāś Bhāg Sanskār*.[12] Although this book of order failed to attract a significant following, the Singh Sabha and its theologians should certainly not be judged on this basis alone. The complexity of its rubrics testifies to the distance which separated most of them from the Panth in general, but the ideals which they developed nevertheless took firm root amongst the educated and from there they have spread to a much larger sector of Sikh society. The order promulgated for the Anand marriage ceremony remains their most impressive success in this regard.

The thrust of the Tat Khalsa attempt to define Sikh identity was strongly towards the exclusive claims of the Khalsa definition and this impulse is clearly represented in *Guramat Prakāś Bhāg Sanskār*. All who participated in its preparation and revision were Khalsa Sikhs[13] and the actual orders for the various rituals are at least implicitly Khalsa in content. Apart from the order for Khalsa initiation, however, it leaves the way open for Sahaj-dhari use of the rites which it prescribes and this was the ultimate legacy of the Singh Sabha period.[14] Kahn Singh explicitly accepts the Sahaj-dhari status, his one condition being that all who claim it should acknowledge only the Guru Granth Sahib as sacred scripture.[15] A place was found for Sahaj-dharis within the general pattern of Khalsa dominance by translating *sahaj* as 'slow'. 'Sahaj-dhari' could thus be construed to mean 'slow-adopter', one who is on his way to the full-fledged Khalsa identity.

By 1915 the Singh Sabha reformers had succeeded in shaping a firmer definition of Sikh identity and in persuading a substantial proportion of educated Sikhs to accept that definition. Two major claims had been

[12] Published from Amritsar, with subsequent reprints.

[13] *Guramat Prakāś Bhāg Sanskār* (1952 edn.), app. 1–3.

[14] The order for the conduct of Sikh funerals distinguishes the Amrit-dhari from other Sikhs in terms which may indicate that the authors had Sahaj-dharis in mind. Ibid. 47.

[15] Kahn Singh Nabha, *Guruśabad ratanākar mahān koś* (2nd rev. edn., Patiala, 1960), 103. In a subsequent revision (published after his death) Kahn Singh strengthened this acceptance of Sahaj-dhari status by adding that 'Singhs who treat Sahaj-dharis with contempt are ignorant of the Sikh religion'. Ibid. 103n. He also included in the plate entitled 'Pictures of Nanak-panthis' a bearded figure labelled 'Sahaj-dhari Sikh'. Ibid., facing p. 518.

lodged and vigorously defended. First, Sikhs are not Hindus. Secondly, a true Sikh will normally be a Sikh of the Khalsa. As a result of their efforts a restored and redefined Khalsa identity had been effectively promulgated, carrying with it the clear implication that only the Khalsa of Singh Sabha definition could be regarded as orthodox.

It was, however, an interpretation which stopped short of any claim to exclusive possession of the entire Panth. Although their role and numbers within the Panth had been significantly diminished, a place still had to be found for Sahaj-dhari Sikhs. The direction of Singh Sabha doctrine might be clearly set towards a complete merging of the terms 'Khalsa' and 'Panth', but that result had not yet been achieved. Moreover, the Singh Sabha reformers had failed to deal adequately with the relationship of the Kes-dhari Sikh to a Panth increasingly defined in Khalsa terms. The definition of a Sikh, clearer now than it had ever been during the past two centuries, was still open to uncertainty and continuing debate.

If the Singh Sabha reformers could afford to be fuzzy at the edges of their definition, no such luxury was available to British administrators charged with framing laws and regulations based on communal distinctions. Apart from occasional issues such as a disputed will, there was the recurrent question of how the decennial census was to be conducted. If religious affiliations were to be returned (an obvious question for any British administrator to include), the census enumerators would have to be supplied with clear definitions of each acceptable identity. Who, in other words, was to be entered as a Sikh when answering census questions?

The initial British definition had been that of the army authorities for whom Sikh did indeed mean Khalsa. In the preliminary Punjab census Sikhs were included as Hindus, but from 1868 onwards they were listed separately.[16] No clear definition was supplied until the 1891 census, when enumerators were instructed to return as Sikhs those who followed the Khalsa order. The practical tests were to be uncut hair and abstinence from smoking. The definition thus implied the Amrit-dhari identity but in practice opted for the more general Kes-dhari form. Sahaj-dharis who failed either of the tests could return their sect as Nanak-panthi or identify themselves as followers of other Sikh Gurus.[17]

Ten years later the same model was adopted except that sects were not

---

[16] Kenneth W. Jones, 'Religious Identity and the Indian Census', in N. Gerald Barrier (ed.), *The Census in British India* (New Delhi, 1981), 79.

[17] Kapur, *Sikh Separatism*, p. 26.

included in the returns.[18] By 1911, however, it was realized that the 1891 tests were being generally ignored and it was accordingly decided to enter as a Sikh every person who claimed to be one. A new category, that of 'Sikh–Hindu', was also permitted. The same procedure was repeated in 1921,[19] clearly implying that, although administrators are meant to be neat and precise, this particular tangle had proven to be too daunting to unravel.

If that was the conclusion reached by the census commissioners, circumstances were already beginning to force the British back to the task of drafting a legal definition of who should be regarded as a Sikh. By 1921 the so-called Gurdwara Reform Movement was already under way and it was to continue until the British authorities eventually conceded that the principal Sikh gurdwaras should be transferred from their hereditary incumbents (the mahants) to elected representatives of the Panth.[20] Elections require voters, and individuals qualify as voters in accordance with specific criteria. Having accepted that such a transfer should indeed take place, the British were again confronted by the need to define a Sikh in statutory terms, and this time they were unable to evade the responsibility.

The history of gurdwara development and administration during the eighteenth and early nineteenth centuries is an obscure one. As we have already noted, the eighteenth-century gurdwara was distinguished from the less impressive dharamsala.[21] Routine kirtan was conducted in the latter, the term 'gurdwara' being reserved for shrines associated with particular events in the lives of the Gurus. Harimandir in Amritsar had become the Panth's principal gurdwara during the course of the eighteenth century. This rank it achieved in intimate association with Akal Takhat, the immediately adjacent gurdwara which symbolized temporal authority within the Panth. During the eighteenth century three other gurdwaras had received the title of *takhat* or 'throne' in recognition of their special role as repositories of Sikh tradition. The actual process whereby these four came to be regarded as takhats is not at all clear, except in the case of Akal Takhat.[22] Akal Takhat may have already

---

[18] Ibid. 26–7.   [19] Ibid. 27.

[20] The history of this episode is narrated in ibid., chaps. 4–6; and Mohinder Singh, *The Akali Movement* (Delhi, 1978).   [21] See chap. 4, n. 42.

[22] The other three are Harimandir in Patna Sahib (where Guru Gobind Singh was born), Kesgarh Sahib in Anandpur (where he instituted the Khalsa), and Hazur Sahib in Nander (where he died). The fifth takhat, Damdama Sahib, which was not definitively designated until 1963, nevertheless surfaced from time to time as a candidate in the early years of the twentieth century. As such it lends some support to the view that the status of the takhat was still a matter of some uncertainty in the Singh Sabha period.

acquired its strongly symbolic identity and it certainly served as venue for the biannual gatherings of the Sarbat Khalsa during the eighteenth-century period of loose confederation.

This same lack of clarity applies to virtually all gurdwaras during the course of the eighteenth century. They were obviously regarded as appropriate destinations for pilgrims and some attracted pious donations from affluent or influential Sikhs.[23] It is, however, a very misty image which they present. Only with the provision of land grants and other privileges do they begin to emerge from obscurity, and they emerge in a form which was later to attract severe disapproval from the Singh Sabha reformers.

Most gurdwaras were in the hands of hereditary mahants and many of these proprietors were able to direct gurdwara income to whatever purposes they might choose. These purposes were not necessarily those which devout convention would approve and one of the standard complaints of reformers during the Singh Sabha period concerned the misappropriation of gurdwara funds. In some instances the income of a gurdwara was evidently directed to personal enrichment, and a few mahants adopted life-styles which piety could only regard as grossly immoral. Under the British their position was further reinforced by the granting of actual titles. In the eyes of the law they had become the owners of their gurdwaras and as such they were entitled to whatever protection the law might provide.[24]

The sins of the mahants were greatly compounded in the eyes of the reformers by the fact that so many of them declined to accept the Khalsa identity. Many described themselves as Udasi Sikhs, a claim which may once have had some justification but which survived as a relic rather than as a genuine identity. The usual assumption is that during the turmoil of the early eighteenth century Sikhs of the Khalsa were too conspicuous to serve as gurdwara custodians, and that later in the century they were too busy establishing Khalsa dominance. They accordingly left the care and conduct of their shrines to Nanak-panthis, who, because they declined to observe Khalsa standards, could hope to escape the hostile attentions of Mughals or Afghans. The preferred candidates were Udasis, celibate followers of the ascetic tradition established (so its adherents claimed) by Guru Nanak's son Siri Chand.[25]

If these assumptions are correct, it follows that the Udasi custodians

---

[23] W. H. McLeod (trans.), *The Chaupā Siṅgh Rahit-nāmā* (Dunedin, 1987), 222.

[24] Teja Singh, *Essays in Sikhism* (Lahore, 1944), 175 ff.

[25] Kapur, *Sikh Separatism*, pp. 43–4.

must soon have abandoned their ascetic obligations, taken wives, and lived as ordinary Hindus. This was the usual life-style of the mahants who so offended the Singh Sabha reformers. The manner in which the mahants conducted gurdwara ritual also caused great offence. No acknowledged standards seemed to exist and the actual practice appeared to be strongly influenced by Hindu example. Amongst other objectionable features, this typically included a refusal to admit outcastes. Drastic reform was obviously needed if the gurdwaras were to serve their intended purpose in the life of the Panth.

In the event, however, the Singh Sabha reformers directed very little of their effective attention to the costly business of seeking a major change in gurdwara control. The Chief Khalsa Diwan had much to be proud of in social and educational terms, and it played a considerable part in bringing educated Sikhs closer together by means of newspaper journalism.[26] With regard to places of worship, however, they concentrated their attention on rituals, seeking to eliminate features which could be regarded as 'Hindu' and particularly those which implied idolatry. In 1905 a famous Tat Khalsa victory was won when idols were removed from the precincts of the Golden Temple,[27] but, apart from a continuing demand for ritual reform, the administration of the mahants was only occasionally challenged.

In thus retaining effective control the mahants had the implicit backing of the British authorities in the Punjab. The alternative, it seemed, would be Tat Khalsa control and this would obviously be unwelcome. A request for representative control of the Golden Temple, received from the Chief Khalsa Diwan in 1906, was ignored.[28] The Golden Temple was to remain under effective government control and mahants were to serve the same purpose in other major gurdwaras.

This eventually proved to be a mistaken policy. Because it involved resistance by government to a popular demand, it attracted a range of protest much wider than the ostensible issue would otherwise have attracted. The ostensible issue was one which could be powerfully represented in traditional terms and as such it could attract dedicated support. The Tat Khalsa claim which had received comparatively little attention or practical support during the first two decades of the twentieth century came dramatically to life after the First World War. A variety of new problems had arisen and the gurdwara issue provided a natural focus for the discontent which they were generating.

---

[26] N. Gerald Barrier, 'The Sikhs and Punjab Politics, 1882–1922'.
[27] Ibid.   [28] Kapur, *Sikh Separatism*, pp. 47–8.

A foretaste of the strife to come was supplied by the protests which followed the government decision to appropriate a portion of the land attached to Gurdwara Rakabganj in order to achieve a desired street alignment during the planning of New Delhi.[29] This occurred in 1912, and, although the restoration campaign was effectively suspended during the war, it eventually provided a preview of later strategies. Meanwhile a host of new issues had developed. These included the growing pressure on many Punjabi cultivators,[30] the grievances of many Sikh migrants to North America, and economic difficulties following the conclusion of the war. Elsewhere in India a new nationalist phase was developing with the agitation against the Rowlatt Bills and when General Dyer opened fire in Jallianwala Bagh the Punjab situation became a major feature of Gandhi's campaign.

Gandhi was able to attract Sikh support for the Non-co-operation Campaign launched in 1920, but for the most part this support was supplied under auspices which were visibly and self-consciously Sikh. The Lucknow Pact of 1916 had not included the Sikhs and in 1917 the Chief Khalsa Diwan, acting under Tat Khalsa pressure, demanded separate electorates for Sikhs. Once again the identity issue was being forced into the legislative arena. Hindu politicians (including those who dominated the Congress Party in the Punjab) objected vigorously, with the result that politics in the Punjab assumed a stronger communal colouring. Tat Khalsa leaders responded by re-emphasizing their Sikh identity and their objections to Hindu practices within the Panth. The gurdwaras were associated with such practices and were accordingly drawn into the developing struggle.[31]

In 1918 the Montagu–Chelmsford Report conceded the claim for separate Sikh electorates and it was subsequently decided that the pragmatic definition of a Sikh would have to serve the purpose of determining the voter roll. Anyone claiming to be a Sikh 'and being prima facie what he represents himself to be' would be entitled to register on the Sikh roll.[32] The continuing controversy relating to this issue persuaded a group of Sikh politicians to found the Sikh League in 1919. The Sikh League endorsed the Congress decision to initiate non-co-operation in 1920, but it was soon superseded by organizations which

---

[29] Khushwant Singh, *A History of the Sikhs*, ii. 196–7.

[30] This particular issue is isolated and extensively discussed by Richard G. Fox in *Lions of the Punjab: Culture in the Making* (Berkeley and Los Angeles, 1985), especially in chaps. 3 and 4.

[31] Kapur, *Sikh Separatism*, pp. 70–6.

[32] Report of the Southborough Committee cited by Kapur, p. 79.

better expressed Tat Khalsa objectives. These were the Shiromani Gurdwara Parbandhak Committee (the SGPC) and its political associate, the Shiromani Akali Dal. Both were founded in late 1920.[33]

The Tat Khalsa now confronted the British, its demand supported by a considerable number of Sikhs (particularly rural Jats) and its campaign waged in alliance with Gandhi and the Congress Party. The objective of the campaign was eviction of the mahants from the gurdwaras which they controlled, and this purpose was kept steadily in view until it was finally achieved in 1925. Although the aim was thus a demonstrably religious one, a varied range of grievances had contributed to the formation of the movement's support, and in accepting Gandhi's non-violent strategy its leaders acknowledged their connection with the larger political campaign. The movement represented a continuation of the old Tat Khalsa purpose, significantly changed in terms of the following which it attracted and of the methods which it used.[34] As such it was appropriate that the Tat Khalsa leaders should form new organizations and that thereafter they should be known as Akalis.[35]

In the midst of these changes the identity issue persisted. The British soon found that the problem had become even more acute, for, having decided that the Akali demand would need to be conceded, they were compelled to negotiate a definition of Sikh identity which could be written into the empowering legislation. Amongst the Sikhs themselves a process already well advanced was accelerating. The Singh Sabha reformers had achieved considerable success with their insistence that the Khalsa should be recognized as the orthodox form of the Panth. The Akali movement further strengthened this claim, infusing it with a new version of the old heroic tradition. Although the Akalis may have

[33] Kapur, *Sikh Separatism*, pp. 82–100. Mohnder Singh, *The Akali Movement*, pp. 87–92. For the SGPC, see Gobinder Singh, *Religion and Politics in the Punjab* (New Delhi, 1986). For the Akali Dal, see Kailash Chander Gulati, *The Akalis Past and Present* (New Delhi, 1974).

[34] For a useful analysis of the relationship with Gandhi and the adoption of non-violent methods, see Partha N. Mukherji, 'Akalis and Violence: An Inquiry into the Theory and Practice of Non-violence', in Amrik Singh (ed.), *Punjab in Indian Politics: Issues and Trends* (Delhi, 1985), 71–118. The article is also of interest for its description of Gandhi's dawning awareness of Sikh identity. 'Till today', he explained to a Gujarati audience in March 1921, 'I had thought of them as a sect of Hinduism. But their leaders think that theirs is a distinct religion.' *The Collected Works of Mahatma Gandhi*, xix. 421, cited by Mukherji, p. 83.

[35] Akali means 'Follower of Akal [Purakh]'. In the eighteenth and early nineteenth century it was a name applied to those who are today called Nihangs. As such it designated one who was particularly ardent in pursuit of religious duties and it was an appropriate choice for the members of the new organization.

adopted a non-violent strategy during this period, they had certainly not parted company with their traditions. Eighteenth-century stories of heroism were invoked and old ideals were proclaimed in an idiom familiar to all nurtured in the Khalsa tradition. The actual events of the Akali campaign need not concern us.[36] What assuredly must concern us is the notable strengthening of Khalsa consciousness which accompanied those events and the definition of a Sikh which was written into the resultant legislation.

As far as the Akalis were concerned, the problem of definition had already been settled by the time the campaign began. When the first elections for the newly established SGPC were held in 1921, voting was restricted to Khalsa Sikhs and all elected members were required to bear the Five Ks.[37] The British eventually accepted a definition which was essentially the same and this was incorporated in the statutory definition of a Sikh written into the Sikh Gurdwaras Act of 1925. Before that point was reached, however, a debate was conducted over the five-year period of the campaign, with the final definition slowly crystallizing as the Akali strategy gradually forced government acceptance of their claims.

There were actually two definitions to be settled during the course of the campaign. In addition to determining who should be regarded as a Sikh, the government was also obliged to define the meaning of 'gurdwara'. Even with the two words 'Sikh' and 'gurdwara' defined to the satisfaction of the Tat Khalsa, there would still remain the question of non-Sikh participation in gurdwara administration. Should gurdwaras be regarded as the exclusive possession of Sikhs, however the latter word might be defined? There were plenty of Punjabi Hindus who stoutly maintained that Hindus were to be numbered amongst the Gurus' ardent devotees and that they, as regular and devout participants in gurdwara worship, were entitled to a share in the administration of the gurdwaras.

The quest for acceptable legislation was begun in 1921 with the introduction into the Punjab Legislative Council of a Sikh Gurdwaras and Shrines Bill. This failed to define either a Sikh or a gurdwara, but during the committee stage a definition was produced for the latter term. A gurdwara was to be defined as 'a Sikh place of public worship erected by or in memory of or in commemoration of any incident in the life of any

---

[36] In addition to Mohinder Singh and Kapur the early events can be followed in part in the older work by Teja Singh, *The Gurdwara Reform Movement and the Sikh Awakening* (Jullundur, 1922; 2nd edn., Amritsar, 1984). Fox's *Lions of the Punjab* is also principally concerned with this period.

[37] Kapur, *Sikh Separatism*, p. 124.

of the ten Sikh Gurus'.[38] This, of course, left 'Sikh' undefined and so too did a second bill introduced in 1922. The 1922 draft did, however, indicate that official opinion was moving down the track laid by the Tat Khalsa, for changes which it incorporated signalled that Tat Khalsa representatives would dominate the board of commissioners which was to control the gurdwaras.

Meanwhile, those who supported the Tat Khalsa cause continued to strengthen their grip on Sikh political activity. The SGPC elections held in July 1923 were again confined to Khalsa Sikhs, and in September of the same year the newly elected members agreed that the SGPC should sponsor candidates for both central and provincial legislatures. All who accepted nomination were to be Amrit-dharis who wore the Five Ks.[39]

The Akali campaign was finally terminated by the drafting and passing of the Sikh Gurdwaras Act of 1925. Chapter 1 of the Act defined a Sikh as 'a person who professes the Sikh religion', adding that the following declaration should be required if any doubt should arise: 'I solemnly affirm that I am a Sikh, that I believe in the Guru Granth Sahib, that I believe in the Ten Gurus, and that I have no other religion.'[40] No attempt was made to define 'gurdwara'. Instead a list of shrines to be covered by the Act was included, together with provision for having others added on appeal.[41] Committees of management were to be variously elected for individual gurdwaras of specified clusters,[42] and a central board was to be constituted for the purpose of general supervision. Of its 151 members, 31 were to be ex officio, nominated, or co-opted. The remaining 120 were to be elected by Sikhs who had passed the age of 21.[43]

As Rajiv Kapur points out, the key phrase in the definition of a Sikh is the concluding portion of the statutory declaration. Those whose Sikh identity might be questioned were required by the declaration to affirm that they had 'no other religion',[44] a form of words which supported the Tat Khalsa claim that Sikhs are not Hindus. For Sahaj-dhari Sikhs this could undoubtedly pose a serious problem, for many of them did indeed

[38] Ibid. 121.

[39] Ibid. 178.

[40] The Sikh Gurdwaras Act 1925, 2(9).

[41] Ibid. 7–17. The wording of the appeals made it clear that the term would not be limited to shrines associated with the Gurus. It could include shrines associated with celebrated Sikhs or important incidents and also those which had been established for public worship without reference to any particular person or event. Ibid. 16(2).

[42] Ibid. 85.

[43] Ibid. 43, 49.

[44] Kapur, *Sikh Separatism*, p. 187.

regard themselves as both Sikh and Hindu. Yet it was not the end of the affair, and, although Kapur rightly emphasizes these three words, he attributes to the Act a clarity and a finality which it did not possess. Although a Tat Khalsa interpretation of the Act would doubtless maintain that its definition of a Sikh necessarily implies the Khalsa identity, the Act does not specify this. A significant loophole remained.

There is, moreover, no sufficient reason for the conclusion which Kapur draws from the Act's reference to Patit Sikhs. The Act debarred Patit Sikhs from membership of individual committees or the central board and this provision, he maintains, automatically disqualified all non-Kes-dhari Sikhs.[45] This is certainly not a legitimate inference. The term *patit* ('fallen', apostate) applies to Amrit-dhari Sikhs who have committed any of the four gross offences specified in the Rahit (notably the cutting of hair or the use of tobacco). It can never apply to a Sahaj-dhari, nor can it strictly apply to an uninitiated Kes-dhari. Its inclusion certainly strengthened the Khalsa colouring of the Act, but it did not finally close the Khalsa circle.

After the passing of the 1925 Act, interest in Sikh affairs quickly receded and throughout the remainder of the British period little notice was taken of the Panth or of its politicians. This did not mean that they were in-active.[46] During the negotiations leading to independence, Sikh claims were pressed by Akali leaders (notably by Master Tara Singh) in an idiom which sustained the close connection between political objectives and Khalsa identity. The central board constituted by the 1925 Act had mean-while decided to retain the name Shiromani Gurdwara Parbandhak Committee and this new SGPC was soon involved in the task of redefining the Rahit. A sub-committee convened by Professor Teja Singh of Amritsar was appointed to review the beliefs and customary practices of the Panth and to prepare a statement for the SGPC to consider.[47] On 1 October 1932 a draft document was duly submitted and after it had been publicly issued for discussion numerous submissions were received. Following a round of further discussions in 1936 the project was evidently shelved until after the Second World War. In early 1945 it was again revived and after some minor amending the sub-committee's proposed text was adopted by the SGPC on 3 February 1945.[48]

---

[45] Ibid.

[46] K. L. Tuteja, *Sikh Politics (1920–40)* (Kurukshetra, 1984), 135–207.

[47] This sub-committee included amongst its twenty-five regular members Kahn Singh Nabha, Vir Singh, and Jodh Singh.

[48] *Sikh Rahit Maryādā* (16th edn., Amritsar, 1983), 1–4. Although a lengthy delay occurred before the approved version was finally issued, an English translation of the draft

The statement thus prepared and formally approved was eventually published by the SGPC in 1950 under the title *Sikh Rahit Maryādā*. In terms of organization it had not been well drafted, particularly with regard to its curious distinction between 'personal discipline' (*śakhasī rahinī*) and 'panthic discipline' (*panthak rahinī*). It is, however, eminently clear as far as most of its definitions and rubrics are concerned. Ambiguity does occur at certain key points, but, as we shall see, this was evidently deliberate.

Whatever faults may be found with *Sikh Rahit Maryādā*, the manual has certainly stood the test of time, assuming since 1950 the status of sole standard authority within the Panth. Apart from the addition of a fifth takhat (Damdama Sahib) to the four recognized in the earlier tradition, its text remains unchanged.[49] By 1983 a total of 178,000 copies of the Punjabi text had been printed and English translations are also available.[50] As a statement of orthodox Sikh belief and normative Sikh conduct, it now stands virtually unchallenged. Although one may certainly encounter a wide range of unsanctioned doctrine and behaviour, the manual itself has no effective rival.

Sikh Rahit Maryādā begins by defining a Sikh. This it does in the following terms: 'A Sikh is any person who believes in Akal Purakh; in the ten Gurus (Guru Nanak to Guru Gobind Singh); in Sri Guru Granth Sahib, other writings of the ten Gurus, and their teachings; in the Khalsa initiation ceremony instituted by the tenth Guru; and who does not believe in any other system of religious doctrine.'[51] The new element is at once obvious. Amongst the items established by earlier convention there now appears the requirement that to be a Sikh one must believe in the Khalsa initiation (*amrit*). Does this mean that the Khalsa circle has finally been closed, that to be a Sikh one must be a member of the Khalsa?

At first sight this would seem to be the obvious conclusion to draw. A closer scrutiny will suggest, however, that such an assumption is still premature. The wording has obviously been chosen with great care, and,

had been published by Teja Singh in his *Sikhism: Its Ideals and Institutions* in 1938. As in all of Teja Singh's works, it is important that the Singh Sabha character of this book should be clearly recognized.

[49] See chap. 6, n. 22.

[50] Two English translations have been published under the title *Rehat Maryada: A Guide to the Sikh Way of Life*, one by Kanwaljit Kaur and Indarjit Singh (London, 1971) and an anonymous version issued by the SGPC (Amritsar, 1978). Neither adheres strictly to the authoritative Punjabi text. An abbreviated version is given in W. H. McLeod (trans.), *Textual Sources for the Study of Sikhism* (Manchester, 1984), 79–86.

[51] *Sikh Rahit Maryādā*, p. 8.

although it is certainly saying that the Khalsa form should be the standard version of the Sikh identity, it does not yet disqualify those who are outside the Khalsa. One is required to 'believe in' (jo ... nisachā rakhdā) the need to take amrit. This form of words, strictly interpreted, can be construed to mean that, whereas a devout Sikh will certainly be expected to take amrit and assume the full range of Khalsa obligations, it is not an essential step. The essential requirement is that one should affirm the value of so doing. This will imply an intention to seek initiation at some time in the future, but it will not automatically deregister all who refrain from taking that step.

The form of words thus used to express the Khalsa aspect of Sikh identity is one which should accommodate the Kes-dhari Sikh without serious difficulty. The Kes-dhari demonstrates his or her attachment to Khalsa norms by maintaining its most conspicuous feature and for this reason can presumably be regarded as someone who believes in the virtue of proceeding to full Khalsa membership. The wording may also be construed as approval of the Sahaj-dhari form, provided only that the 'slow-adopter' definition is upheld and that the Sahaj-dhari can accordingly be viewed as someone progressing towards full participation in the Khalsa. Some stricter members of the Khalsa do indeed interpret the amrit reference as a mandatory obligation, one which allows no evasion or fudging. It appears, however, that this was not the view of Professor Teja Singh while drafting Sikh Rahit Maryādā, and it was certainly not the interpretation accepted by Kahn Singh Nabha.[52]

Sikh Rahit Maryādā is also ambiguous with regard to the precise status of the Patit Sikh, the 'apostate' or 'renegade' Amrit-dhari who wilfully commits any of the four gross sins (the chār kurahit).[53] Is a Patit still a Sikh or do these offences produce automatic excommunication? The wording which is actually used in references to the Patit seems to imply that offenders are indeed still Sikhs. It is, however, debatable. They are certainly not members of the Khalsa (this is made clear by the requirement that repentance must be followed by re-initiation) and the clear indication that the mere presence of a Patit is polluting signifies a very strong condemnation.[54] But are they to be altogether stripped of their Sikh identity? This seems not to be the case, although doubtless there will be a fundamentalist interpretation of this point also.

---

[52] Teja Singh, Sikhism: Its Ideals and Institutions (rev. edn., 1951), 84. Kahn Singh Nabha, Gurumat mārtaṇḍ (Amritsar, 1962), 111–14.

[53] Sikh Rahit Maryādā, p. 26.

[54] Ibid. 26, 27.

This combination of Khalsa norms and ambiguously implied exceptions informs *Sikh Rahit Maryādā* as a whole. Its version of Ardas (the so-called 'Sikh Prayer') includes repeated references to the Khalsa, yet it concludes with an eirenic couplet which gathers all people into a single blessing.[55] The Khalsa flag (*niśān sāhib*) is to fly above all gurdwaras, but access is open to all apart from particularly sacred areas within the takhats.[56] A reference in the order for the Anand marriage service seems plainly to imply that all Sikhs are not Amrit-dharis.[57] The funeral order, however, assumes that the deceased will have observed the Five Ks.[58] Whereas the 'Panth' consists of Sikhs, the 'Guru Panth' is limited to 'full-fledged Singhs' (*tiār-bar-tiār siṅgh*).[59]

Although the ambiguity persists, the question of orthodoxy is put beyond all doubt. As far as the SGPC is concerned, standard belief and practice are defined by the Khalsa Rahit, and if others are to be accepted as Sikhs they should aspire to full membership of the Khalsa. But is the SGPC the ultimate authority, and must its pronouncements be accepted as the final word on any issue concerning doctrine and practice? Authority is one of the problems which still remains to be considered before we finally attempt to define who is a Sikh.[60]

Before concluding this narrative of the attempt to define Sikh identity by legislation, we should note one further contribution. When India became independent in 1947, the Punjab inherited the Sikh Gurdwaras Act of 1925 as a part of the legislative bequest from the British period. The Act is still in force and the definition of 'Sikh' which it enunciated remains unamended. It is, however, an Act which applies only to the Punjab and immediately adjacent territories. Because the gurdwaras of Delhi and New Delhi were beyond its jurisdiction, fresh legislation was required in order to regularize their administration.

The need for an act of Parliament to cover the Delhi territory gurdwaras provided yet another opportunity for the debate to recommence in earnest. Although it is by no means clear who exercised the determining influence, or for what reasons, the outcome was certainly an interesting one. In the course of 1971 two such Acts were passed by the Lok Sabha. The first of these was the Delhi Gurdwara (Management) Act 24 of 1971 and, in this first attempt to settle the issue, the word 'Sikh'

[55] Ibid. 10.
[56] Ibid. 12, 13.
[57] Ibid. 21.
[58] Ibid.
[59] Ibid. 23.
[60] See chap. 7.

was defined in terms closely following those of the 1925 Act.[61] The later Act significantly amended this definition. In the Delhi Gurdwara Act 82 of 1971 a Sikh is defined as follows:

'Sikh' means a person who professes the Sikh religion, believes and follows the teachings of Sri Guru Granth Sahib and the ten Gurus only *and keeps unshorn hair*. For the purposes of this Act, if any question arises as to whether any living person is or is not a Sikh, he shall be deemed respectively to be or not to be a Sikh according as he makes or refuses to make in the manner prescribed by rules the following declaration:—

'I solemnly affirm that I am a *Keshadhari* Sikh, that I believe in and follow the teachings of Sri Guru Granth Sahib and, the ten Gurus only, and that I have no other religion.'[62]

Between the two Acts a successful attempt had evidently been made to narrow the definition in such a way that Sahaj-dharis would be explicitly deprived of any right to call themselves Sikhs. It is clear, however, that there was no intention of limiting the definition to Amrit-dhari Sikhs. The chosen wording specifically enfranchises the Kes-dhari.

There is no reason why this piece of legislation should be regarded as representative of Sikh opinion in general, nor that it would necessarily have secured SGPC approval had that been invited. Legislation may well reflect the temporary influence of a particular pressure group and there seems to be little doubt that the second of these Acts should be regarded as an example of this effect.[63] Although this should certainly be acknowledged, it does not entitle us to dismiss the episode or its result as an issue of little consequence. It confronts us yet again with the central problem and with the importance which the problem commands. Who is a Sikh? A final attempt must be made to answer the question.

---

[61] Attar Singh, 'The Management of Gurudwaras' in Amrik Singh (ed.), *Punjab in Indian Politics*, p. 199.

[62] Quoted in ibid. The text is contained in Jitinder Kaur, *The Politics of Sikhs: A Study of Delhi Sikh Gurdwara Management Committee* (New Delhi, 1986), 242. The emphasis to *and keeps unshorn hair* was added by Attar Singh.

[63] Jitinder Kaur, *The Politics of Sikhs*, pp. 34–5.

Who is a Sikh?

IT WOULD be most convenient if there were to be an acknowledged authority, some individual or assembly to whom we might appeal for a clear and certain answer to our question 'Who is a Sikh?' Definitions are readily available and willingly dispensed, yet basic disagreements persist and the indisputable answer still seems to elude us.

There is, of course, one authority which most Sikhs will instantly cite. The Adi Granth, visible embodiment of the eternal Guru, is the divine Word which all devout Sikhs must accept and none may challenge. Its status is indeed beyond dispute, yet even this response must fail to answer our question, at least in terms sufficiently detailed to settle the issue in its present form. The Guru Granth Sahib will supply us with some basic features of the definition which we seek, and at least one of those features must be incorporated in any definition which we may finally present. This we must acknowledge without accepting the claim that it can deliver anything resembling a complete answer to our question. The Adi Granth was compiled prior to the founding and subsequent development of the Khalsa and, as we have repeatedly observed, any attempt to define Sikh identity must certainly take account of the Khalsa contribution. In this regard the Adi Granth may indicate some appropriate lines of enquiry, but it cannot be expected to supply the kind of answer which we require.

The one essential feature which the Adi Granth does provide derives from its emphasis on the doctrine of the divine Name. Guru Nanak and his early successors leave us in no doubt that for them this is the one fundamental belief which all must accept. The divine Name is the substance of truth and the practice of *nām simaraṇ* is the one assured means of liberation from the cycle of transmigration. The doctrine of the divine Name must accordingly be built into any adequate definition of Gurmat (or what we call, when speaking English, Sikhism). From this it follows that a definition of the person who accepts Gurmat must likewise include some reference to the divine Name and to the duty of regular *nām simaraṇ*.[1]

[1] See chap. 2.

We shall indeed include both the doctrine and the duty in our final definition, but let us be aware of the difficulties which it adds to our basic problem of framing that definition. It would be idle to suggest that all who regard themselves as Sikhs have a clear understanding of the Adi Granth doctrine of the divine Name or that they regularly practise anything resembling the technique of *nām simaraṇ* as enunciated by Guru Nanak and his successors. For many it will be acknowledged as nothing more than an occasional utterance of the pious ejaculation *Sati-nām* ('True is the Name'), while for others it will exist as a word recollected from childhood or as someone's personal name. A close acquaintance with the actual contents of the Guru Granth Sahib is not a feature of Sikh life which we should expect to encounter with any frequency. To assume it would be as unrealistic as imagining that all who call themselves Christians have a reasonable understanding of the Bible and its contents.

The two situations are very similar, for in both cases we are dealing with traditions which seek a measure of doctrinal precision. In examining the extent to which the Adi Granth is actually comprehended by Sikhs we are inevitably confronted by the problem of nominal identity as opposed to devout observance. Our task would be considerably eased by a decision to confine ourselves to the latter, concentrating our attention on a quest for the normative version of the tradition. It is, however, a temptation which should be resisted. A close analysis of the normative version is essential, but alone it is insufficient. It would lead us to an ideal rather than to a reality, to a definition which excludes many who regard themselves as Sikhs or to one which implicitly brands them as 'bad' Sikhs.

This decision complicates our task without eliminating the need for normative statements or the problem of identifying an acceptable authority within the Panth. The problem recurs when we proceed to examine the second of the standard answers to the general question of authority. Within the Panth the only organization which can claim representative status is the Shiromani Gurdwara Parbandhak Committee (the SGPC), and on occasion the SGPC has acted as if it were indeed an ultimate authority. Should this assumption of doctrinal power be accepted?

Most members of the SGPC are elected by popular vote of all who can establish their Sikh credentials in terms of the 1925 Sikh Gurdwaras Act.[2] This restricts the electorate to the Punjab and adjacent territories,

[2] Gobinder Singh, *Religion and Politics in the Punjab* (New Delhi, 1986), 79–85.

but a verdict delivered from the acknowledged heartland of the Sikhs is surely one to be respected by those who happen to live elsewhere. The SGPC has assumed the right to act as an ultimate authority in matters of doctrine and religious practice as well as in issues which more narrowly concern the administration of gurdwaras. *Sikh Rahit Maryādā* was prepared under its auspices and issued with its imprimatur. If *Sikh Rahit Maryādā* is to be accepted as an authoritative manual of Sikh doctrine and behaviour, it must surely follow that the SGPC is to be acknowledged as a court of final appeal in all matters relating to Sikh belief.

In practice this claim was widely rejected even before the present crisis, particularly amongst the educated and professional élites within the Panth. If one had asked a well-educated Sikh what he or she thought of the SGPC, the response was likely to be a prompt rejection of its claims to virtue, intelligence, or authority. Money was commonly identified as the culprit and politics as the curse which it conferred. Because the SGPC had access to such enormous funds through its control of gurdwara incomes, it offered an irresistible temptation to those who seek power and status. These funds it used (so the claim continued) to support a retinue of dependants within the gurdwaras themselves and an unstable programme of political action in the wider world of the Punjab.[3]

Even before the troubles of the middle and late 1980s these views were widespread. What opinions are held now would be difficult to ascertain, but it is safe to assume that the intellectual leadership of the Panth rejects the SGPC's right to pronounce on questions of doctrine and practice. There also appears to be abundant evidence which suggests that many more Sikhs see the SGPC as an essentially political body. It is conceived as a political organization, currently one which is in the hands of a distinctly militant group. As such it is certainly not one which can claim to determine religious principles which will carry weight in the Panth as a whole. This is not to say that the SGPC is devoid of power, nor that the exercise of that power is contrary to the interests of the Panth. That may or may not be the case. The essential fact is that its primary role is political. If it has a religious role, it is to exalt a narrowly Khalsa identity and to frighten away virtually all who would otherwise be prepared to call themselves Sahaj-dhari.

The same rejection is also extended to the so-called 'High Priests' of the Panth, a group of seven men who have received much attention in the recent past because of the use which has been made of them in pursuing

[3] Ibid. 154.

political advantage or settlement during the continuing crisis in the Punjab. The group comprises the Chief Granthis of Darbar Sahib (the Golden Temple) and Akal Takhat, together with the Jathedars or 'Commanders' of all five takhats. In normal circumstances their authority is limited and to call them 'high' is a somewhat doubtful usage. To call them 'priests' is wholly erroneous, for the Sikh tradition acknowledges no such role or authority. During the current crisis their newly bestowed status has been useful to both sides as a means of buttressing their own political strategies or obstructing that of their opponents. As authorities on matters of doctrine or practice their influence is negligible except in so far as they reflect the views of their masters.[4]

Sants supply another source of authority within the Panth, and within the range of an individual Sant's personal following that authority may be considerable. It will be all the stronger if he belongs to an established lineage of venerable repute. The title 'Sant' is in this sense a comparatively modern usage, although the actual role has been recognized within the Panth since the eighteenth century at least. A Sikh Sant is an individual (almost always a male) who develops a reputation for piety or pedagogical skill and thereby attracts an informal following of disciples. Sants are typically the products of rural society (most are Jats) and until recently their influence was largely limited to the villages where they imparted instruction in traditional Sikh doctrine or kirtan.

Because the Khalsa ideal stresses participation in worldly affairs, some Sants have been active in the larger life of the community, and the current participation of Sants in Sikh politics is an extension of this convention. This has significantly enlarged their range of influence during recent years, and so too has the increasingly popular practice of travelling overseas to minister to Sikhs in the diaspora. Amongst the recognized lineages one stands pre-eminent. This is the Damdama Taksal, led by Sant Jarnail Singh Bhindranwale until his death in 1984 during the storming of the Golden Temple complex.[5]

---

[4] W. H. McLeod, 'A Sikh Theology for Modern Times', in J. D. O'Connell *et al*. (eds.), *Sikh History and Religion in the Twentieth Century*, (Toronto, 1988), 42.

[5] Jarnail Singh Bhindranwale died during the army assault on the Golden Temple complex in June 1984. Other Sants who have achieved political prominence in recent times include Sant Fateh Singh of Punjabi Suba fame and the moderate Akali leader Sant Harchand Singh Longowal. For a description of the Sikh Sant and an analysis of his role, see W. H. McLeod, 'The Meaning of *sant* in Punjabi Usage', in Karine Schomer and W. H. McLeod (eds.), *The Sants: Studies in a Devotional Tradition of India* (Berkeley and Delhi, 1987), 251–63; and id., 'The Role of Sikh Doctrine and Tradition in the Current Punjab

Several Sants have achieved substantial influence in recent times and for many generations they have acted as effective mediators of traditional Khalsa attitudes. There are, however, major limits to their influence. Most live and work in the Malwa region (the area south and east of the Satluj River) and few command a following beyond traditional village society. The response which they elicit from most educated Sikhs ranges from tolerant indifference to strong condemnation. It is an important influence which they exercise and it should certainly not be disregarded. There is, however, no prospect that any Sant will be accepted as a final authority, except by those who choose to join his following.

The only other authority recognized within the Panth is that of the corporate community. This may be expressed in two forms, the ambitious version deriving from the doctrine of the Guru Panth and the less prominent from a traditional pattern of delegation within individual sangats.

According to the doctrine of the Guru Panth the assembled community constitutes the Sarbat Khalsa (the 'Entire Khalsa'), and any corporate decision which the Sarbat Khalsa may make in the presence of the Guru Granth Sahib bears the full weight of the eternal Guru's personal authority.[6] The doctrine still stands, but it is extraordinarily difficult to apply in practice. Indeed, it is altogether impossible to implement it in such a way that all Sikhs will acknowledge the outcome. Although attempts have been made to revive the practice in recent years, the doctrine is strictly dysfunctional, a convention which served a useful purpose during the eighteenth century but which has since been immobilized by changed circumstances and the ever-widening diversity of the Panth.

The other version of corporate authority is much less cumbersome and has consequently retained a portion of its original strength. This is the *pañj piāre* convention, the practice of choosing five members of a sangat to act on its behalf.[7] It is, however, a convention which retains its effect only within a comparatively small group of Sikhs, and only when the group is reasonably united in terms of purpose and understanding. Where these conditions are lacking, divisions commonly occur and splinter sangats appear (particularly amongst the more mobile diaspora

---

Crisis', in Jayant K. Lele *et al.* (eds.), *Boeings and Bullock-Carts: Rethinking India's Restructuring* (Leiden, forthcoming).

[6] See above, p. 55.

[7] The practice commemorates Guru Gobind Singh's choosing of five loyal Sikhs to receive the first initiation as members of the Khalsa in 1699.

Sikhs). As a means of decision-making on a large scale it can be effective only when a substantial majority of the Panth is fired by a common concern or a common indignation.

As a single authority exercised on behalf of the entire Panth the convention can seldom, if ever, hope to win general acceptance. Applied within individual sangats it can serve a useful purpose, but only within that sangat or its immediate environment. Each group of *pañj piāre* will normally reflect the attitudes of those who chose them, and the range of opinion which these groups represent will be as diverse as the full spectrum allows. To propose the *pañj piāre* convention as a decision-making system for the Panth as a whole would be a recipe for independency of the Protestant kind.

If, therefore, we seek an authority which will deliver an accurate and sufficient definition of a Sikh, our search will produce several differing results and consequently no result. We note the Adi Granth stress on the divine Name as one part of the final definition and proceed to ask if a consensus view can be identified. Granted that no text, individual, or institution can supply the answer which we need, is it nevertheless possible to isolate particular items which all Sikhs (apart from mavericks and recognized eccentrics) accept as essential features of their own identity? The enterprise is scarcely a promising one, but it may carry us a little nearer to an agreed definition. It can be assumed, for example, that apart from the truly secular all Sikhs will affirm the sanctity of the Guru Granth Sahib. Even the most ardent of secularized Sikhs will recognize this feature by ritually prostrating before the sacred book on the rare occasions when he is compelled to enter its presence.[8]

Entering the presence of the Guru Granth Sahib normally means entering a gurdwara and here we encounter another feature which few Sikhs would dispute. The religious centre for Sikhs is the gurdwara, an institution which wins grudging approval from many of the lax and secularized as well as firm support from the pious. This approval may be hedged with protests concerning the frequency of factional disputes within gurdwaras or their misuse for political purposes, and it may be accompanied by a lofty disdain for the gurdwara's role as a place of worship. Normally, however, the point will be conceded. When Sikhs

---

[8] It should be noted that 'secular' and 'secularized' are here used in the Western sense and thus designate a person who lacks religious convictions. The word 'secular' or its derivatives can cause much confusion if one is unaware of the radical difference between the Western usage and the meaning which the terms have assumed in Indian usage. In the latter context 'secular' typically means 'equal respect for all religions'. A pious practising Sikh (or Hindu, Muslim, Christian, etc.) can accordingly claim to be secular in outlook.

travel to foreign places, they usually find themselves drawn to a gurdwara, and if none should exist the deficiency will soon be remedied.

It is, moreover, recognized that the gurdwara is the place where the egalitarian principles of the Panth are most effectively applied, a feature which appeals to many who reject its devotional role. The langar is a convention which commands universal respect within the Panth and even the secularized can find meaning in the impartial distribution of karah prasad.[9] The same people may also accept the traditional concept of service (*sevā*). The concept may be construed as a kind of social welfare activity rather than the traditional variety,[10] but even that will normally prove acceptable to many of the more pious.

We can thus add reverence for the Guru Granth Sahib and acknowledgement of the gurdwara to the agreed features which together constitute Sikh identity. The gurdwara also directs us to another possibility. Within every gurdwara and during most Sikh ceremonies Ardas (the 'Sikh Prayer') is recited.[11] The structure of Ardas evidently derives from the eighteenth century, although the content of the version used today includes much that belongs to more recent times. Because Ardas is routinely recited in Sikh rituals, we can perhaps assume that its fundamental features should also be added to our list of agreed items. An actual analysis of its contents will soon reveal, however, that our luck is running out again.

The invocation with which Ardas begins calls to mind each of the Gurus by name and this portion of the prayer is surely acceptable to all but the narrowest of Nanak-panthis. Veneration for the Gurus is thus another of the features which can be added to our consensus list. The concluding petition is also likely to find general acceptance, although it adds little that will supplement a distinctive identity.[12] It is when we

---

[9] The langar is the kitchen and refectory attached to every gurdwara from which food is served to all regardless of caste or creed. Karah prasad is the sacramental food dispensed in all gurdwaras, again without reference to the individual's caste or creed.

[10] In a strict sense *sevā* is *sevā* done for the Guru, which in practice means *sevā* performed in the precincts of a gurdwara. Such activities as cleaning the shoes of worshippers, sweeping the sacred premises, and helping in the langar are all typical forms of *sevā*.

[11] For a translation of the version incorporated in *Sikh Rahit Maryādā* and in use today, see W. H. McLeod (trans.), *Textual Sources for the Study of Sikhism* (Manchester, 1984), 104–5. The complete prayer consists of three distinct sections (invocation, recollection, and petition). Only the first eight lines (the invocation) and the concluding couplet are unalterable. There is, however, a standard version for the second section and for most of the third. See ibid. 103–4.

[12] The concluding portion is the portion which begins with the words 'May Sikhs be humble of heart . . .'.

scrutinize the intervening section (the 'remembrance of past mercies') that we recognize the return of old problems. The middle portion is patently a prayer of the Khalsa and, if its text be treated as a statement of essential doctrine, the result must be a reaffirmation of the standard Khalsa interpretation. This portion of Ardas is in fact a product of the Tat Khalsa understanding of Sikh tradition. The element of ambiguity is still retained and determined exegesis may yield an interpretation acceptable to Sahaj-dhari claims. The import is, however, strongly that of the militant Panth and of the Kes-dhari identity.

The consensus approach thus provides some additional items before it runs into the difficulties which emerged during the Singh Sabha and Akali periods. At this point we shall abandon doctrine and try a generic approach to the problem of definition. Claims concerning the nature of Sikh society have been vigorously debated within the Panth and widely proclaimed as vital aspects of Sikh identity. Our next task must be to estimate the results of the debate. It requires us to venture on to distinctly risky ground, but the attempt must nevertheless be made if all aspects of the problem are to be adequately explored.

There are two terms which must be examined in the process of testing popular generic claims and the first of these is 'race'. Can we accept the claim that Sikhs constitute a separate race? The wording of race relations legislation in the United Kingdom has provided a defence for this claim and one can easily understand why Sikhs who wish to combat perceived discrimination should have recourse to the appropriate laws. This does not mean, however, that we must accept the claim in any general or universal sense. It is manifestly impossible to defend the claim that Sikhs are a distinct and separate race, except in the terms imposed by the race relations context in the United Kingdom. The narrowest possible definition will classify them as Punjabis and no one can claim that all Punjabis are Sikhs.

It is likewise impossible to claim that all Sikhs are Punjabis. It is indeed true that an overwhelming majority of Sikhs are Punjabis, and an interesting question with some relevance to our main purpose concerns the failure of the tradition to attract significant numbers of non-Punjabis.[13] No one, however, will deny the possibility that non-Punjabis may join the Panth and actual examples can easily be found. The claim that Sikhs are a distinct race need detain us no longer.

[13] Two suggested reasons may be that in other parts of India Sant teachings required no allegiance to the Nanak-panth (there were other panths which could be joined); and Khalsa symbols and conventions would have been regarded as alien.

The second generic term which we must examine is 'nation' and here we encounter a much knottier problem, one which is liable to generate very strong reactions. Although the first application of the word 'nation' to the Sikhs goes back to the earliest days of British contact, it did not receive significant emphasis until recent times. After the collapse of Ranjit Singh's kingdom, the British themselves used the word very loosely, and throughout the nationalist phase of the British period there was little questioning of the Sikh place within an independent India. Only as the Muslim League claim to nationhood crystallized and produced the threat of partition did the concept of a Sikh 'nation' begin to attract serious attention. Since independence it has designated the extreme version of the popular Sikh claim that the Punjab should receive a larger measure of political autonomy. In times of communal crisis it waxes strongly and in recent years its radical exponents have dramatized the claim as a demand for Khalistan.

There is much to be said in defence of the claim that the Panth constitutes a separate nation. The *mīrī–pīrī* doctrine affirms a political role for the Panth,[14] and the claim can be more generally defended in terms of the distinctive culture which the Panth embodies. There are, however, problems. Those who dispute the notion insist that too much of the Panth's culture is in fact Punjabi culture and that too much of its tradition overlaps with the larger tradition of India as a whole. There is, moreover, the difficulty of demarcating a viable area to be occupied by the Sikh nation, an essential feature of any realistic claim.

This is an argument which will presumably continue for quite some time to come. For present purposes a more realistic approach is to ask whether 'nation' is really the appropriate translation for what many of its more moderate exponents have actually had in mind. There seems to be little doubt that for many Sikhs 'nation' has served as a translation for the word *qaum*. If so, it is a thoroughly misguided choice, one of the many examples of how meanings can be seriously distorted by endeavouring to find single-word translations for terms which have no equivalent in English.

In its original Arabic form *qaum* designates 'a people who stand together' and this meaning has survived its adoption into Punjabi usage. As such it does indeed denote a strong sense of corporate identity and this fact is significant as far as our quest for a definition is concerned. It is nevertheless a meaning which differs from the strict sense of the English

---

[14] The *mīrī* part of the combination designates worldly authority (the authority of the *mīr* or *amīr*, the master of a realm). See above, p. 24.

word 'nation'. Whereas it certainly connotes a strong sense of ethnic identity, it does not bear a precise correspondence to 'nation'. There can be no doubt that some of those who today proclaim the existence of a Sikh nation are using the word in its strictly accurate sense. If, however, the essential content derives from *qaum*, the term should be discarded.

The conclusion must be that our attempt to use the generic approach has largely failed. The sense of a distinct Sikh identity will certainly be strengthened by an analysis of *qaum* in its specifically Sikh usage, but that alone will not serve to supply the distinctive features which we need. In a very real sense our quest has all along been an attempt to discover why Sikhs perceive themselves to be a *qaum*.

We turn next to the pragmatic approach. Regardless of what doctrine may declare or theory may claim, what do we actually see when we scrutinize the Panth?

One issue which we have not yet examined is the place of women in the Panth. The issue is one which concerns doctrines as much as observable behaviour and it might well have been discussed at an earlier stage. In practice, however, actual behaviour is normally much more important than doctrine when dealing with the status of women and for this reason it is generally more helpful to deal with the issue in pragmatic terms.

In theory women are regarded as the equals of men in the Panth. As one might expect, their actual status falls short of the theoretical claim, but this is not to suggest that women possess neither rights nor influence. Their right to participate in panthic rituals is generally recognized, even to the extent of permitting women to sit in attendance on the Guru Granth Sahib and read from the sacred scripture in public worship. Sikhs commonly claim that their women possess a much greater freedom than those who belong to other areas of Indian society. Sweeping assertions of this kind are difficult to test and it might be countered that in Punjabi villages (where most Sikh women live) there is little to distinguish the roles of Hindu and Sikh women belonging to similar castes. It must nevertheless be accepted that prima facie the claim is at least plausible and that as such it deserves to be examined.

The reality, as one would expect from Western experience, is that the actual place of women in the Panth is conspicuously subordinate to that of males. There exists a small élite of educated urban women with access to substantial influence and opportunity, but they are exceptions to a generally consistent rule. Women may take Khalsa initiation and having done so they are expected to observe the same code of conduct as men (with the exception of the turban, which is optional for women and very seldom worn).[15] Whenever the Rahit is discussed, however, or whenever the special claims of the Sikhs are debated, the focus is normally fixed on the male identity with a strong reference to beards and turbans. Those who exercise effective authority within the Panth are almost always men and likewise the various functionaries who serve in gurdwaras. Sants, granthis, jathedars, members of the SGPC—virtually all are men.

It is, of course, possible to exaggerate the difference between male and female influence within the Panth and we should take care not to do so. Against the conspicuous prominence of male participation should be set the strong emphasis which is laid on girls' education, the traditional role of the mother in an Indian household, and the growing number of Sikh women in professional occupations. In many ways the situation is similar to that which Western societies are finally and hesitantly acknowledging. In some respects Sikh women may be starting further back than their Western counterparts, but at least there is clear doctrinal support for equal rights within the Panth.

Caste also presents an apparent conflict between doctrine or theory on the one hand and actual practice on the other.[16] Can a rejection of caste be included in our definition of Sikh identity? The answer has to be both yes and no. In ritual terms and within a gurdwara the answer can certainly be an affirmative, at least since the days of the Singh Sabha and Akali movements. The Khalsa rite of initiation is manifestly anti-caste in intention and involves the drinking of the same *amrit* from a common vessel. Within any gurdwara karah prasad is freely distributed to all, and in its langar all must sit in symbolic lines to receive the same food. Outside the gurdwara the same willingness to eat together is generally observed. Strict Sikhs of the Khalsa may refuse to eat with non-Sikhs,[17] but these same people are often in the vanguard of those who insist on full commensality within the Panth. The first answer to our question must be yes, the Panth does indeed reject caste.

The second answer must be no because within the Panth caste is still generally observed in terms of familial relationships and marriage alliances. Jat marries Jat, Khatri marries Khatri (or at least an Arora or an Ahluwalia), Ramgarhia marries Ramgarhia, and Mazhabi marries Mazhabi. Exceptions can easily be found, but they remain exceptions.

---

[15] *Sikh Rahit Maryādā*, p. 18. The European women who belong to Yogi Bhajan's 3HO following all wear turbans.

[16] For a description and discussion of caste in the Panth, see W. H. McLeod, *The Evolution of the Sikh Community*, (Oxford, 1976), chap. 5.

[17] *Sikh Rahit Maryādā*, p. 27.

Many Sikhs use their caste name as a surname (Singh or Kaur thus becomes a middle name) and political parties can generally depend on caste alignments in Sikh society as much as in Hindu. Even the gurdwara may be affected. Major gurdwaras have generally been immune since the early decades of the present century, but local gurdwaras are commonly the preserve of a single caste (particularly those serving Sikhs overseas). In the case of Ramgarhia gurdwaras, this identity is frequently proclaimed in the actual name. Gurdwaras dominated by other castes are usually more discreet in this respect, but wherever such an identity exists it will be well known to all members of the local community.

Issues requiring both affirmative and negative answers present obvious problems when we are endeavouring to establish an objective and describable identity. If we repeat our question, the accurate answer will presumably have to be that, whereas caste has been largely destroyed in ritual terms, it continues to exercise a fundamental influence on the social and political life of the Panth. Whereas the doctrine of the Panth expressly condemns caste,[18] a substantial majority of Sikhs observe certain significant features of caste in practice.

Although we have travelled a certain distance towards a definition of Sikh identity, we have still managed to avoid the most conspicuous issue of all. None of the items which we have so far managed to elicit from our various questions and approaches concerns the specific Khalsa identity or its relationship to non-Khalsa identities within the Panth. What conclusions are we entitled to draw in this regard when we apply the pragmatic approach? In particular, what results emerge when we scrutinize the actual observance of Amrit-dhari, Kes-dhari, and Sahaj-dhari identities?

A first conclusion is that in actual practice little distinction is drawn between the Amrit-dhari and Kes-dhari modes. Times of crisis (such as the recent past and the present) will typically produce a stronger emphasis on the former and one may find baptismal jathas touring the villages of the Punjab for the express purpose of administering *amrit* to as many people as possible. In normal circumstances, however, it is the visible evidence which matters. Those who retain their hair uncut and refrain from smoking will be accepted as Sikhs if they claim the identity, and for all practical purposes they will be regarded as Sikhs of the Khalsa.

The wearing of the supplementary Khalsa symbols will strengthen any such impression, but few eyes will look for them when credentials are being informally established. The bangle (*kaṛā*) will normally be worn

18 Ibid. 12, 16, 17, 23, 24.

and one may assume that a regulation comb (*kaṅghā*) is concealed beneath the turban. Attached to the comb there may well be a miniature *kirpān*, a tiny replica which serves as a substitute for the real article (except when times of crisis focus a very specific attention on it). The *kachh* likewise presents no problems. The shorts which are actually worn may differ considerably in size and cut from the traditional style, but the actual article is normally concealed from sight and the issue seldom generates any fervour. The beard and tobacco are the two standard tests. Even these two criteria may be disregarded in some circles, though once either line is crossed claims to a Sikh identity will be treated as arguable.

At this point a debate may indeed develop and one aspect of any such debate will bring us back to the question of caste. If a Jat cuts his hair, there is a strong likelihood that his claims to be regarded as a Sikh will continue to be recognized. If, however, any member of the Khatri/Arora/Ahluwalia group should do likewise, he will usually be treated thereafter as a Hindu. The same is also true of Harijan Sikhs except that in their case the alternate identity could conceivably be Christian. Ramgarhias occupy an ambivalent middle ground. If they retain a strong Ramgarhia identity, they will probably be regarded as Sikhs, particularly in overseas communities. For most Ramgarhias the original identity is that of Tarkhan (the carpenter caste) and if the principal Khalsa symbol were to be abandoned the obvious designation in a village situation would be Hindu. We are, however, perilously near guesswork at this point and for the sake of safety we must retreat to the clearer identities of the Jat on the one hand and the Khatri/Arora/Ahluwalia group on the other.

The differing responses of these two groups can be explained in terms of the dominant affiliation in each case. The Jats involved in this comparison are those who live in the Indian state of Punjab or who trace their origins to that area. Jats who live in Pakistan are Muslims and those who reside in Haryana or adjacent Uttar Pradesh are Hindus. Each can be clearly distinguished from those who occupy the intervening territory, and in the case of the Hindu community the caste name changes from *Jat* to *Jāṭ*. Those who occupy Indian Punjab (together with adjacent strips of Haryana and Rajasthan) identify strongly as Sikhs and they retain this affiliation regardless of their level of adherence to the Rahit. The punctilious may reject their claims, but few Jats will accept such a judgement.

We have here entered the one area where a generic claim can actually be sustained. When we move into the society of Khatris, Aroras, and Ahluwalias, the situation changes. Most Khatris and Aroras are Hindus and it is the Hindu affiliation (commonly Arya Samaj) which dictates the dominant tradition. Ahluwalias derive from a different origin, but, because they have chosen to identify closely with Khatris and Aroras, their own traditions have changed accordingly.[19] The perceptions of others have undergone a corresponding change, with the result that Ahluwalias are generally associated with Khatris and Aroras. If a Sikh from any of these three castes should cut his hair, most other people will eventually regard him as a Hindu.

This is an exceedingly complicated situation and it becomes even more complex when we acknowledge (as we must) that Khatris and Aroras who cut their hair or smoke do not necessarily regard themselves as Hindus. They may identify as Sikhs, as Hindus, or as both. This brings us back to the problem of the Sahaj-dhari, a problem which largely concerns the Khatri/Arora sector of the Panth. Is the person who claims to be a Sahaj-dhari actually accepted as a Sikh or is the claim rejected in practice? Present circumstances suggest that three answers can now be given to this question and that one of the three is assuming a strong dominance within the Panth.

The first answer is the old claim that it is possible to be a Sikh without regarding membership of the Khalsa as a necessary or preferred option. Many Punjabi Hindus still affirm this view, but it now has negligible support amongst those who actually identify as Sikhs. The second answer is the Singh Sabha interpretation. This affirms the orthodoxy of the Khalsa mode, but leaves a window open for those who reverence the Guru Granth Sahib without accepting the Rahit. Although this response still commands some support, it seems to attract little enthusiasm today. It seems clear that a substantial majority of those who regard themselves as Sikhs either reject the Sahaj-dhari option completely or treat it as irrelevant.[20] In practice it is now very difficult to find people who explicitly affirm a Sahaj-dhari identity. Changing circumstances may revive the debate in the future, but for the time being it seems to have lapsed.

This does not mean, however, that the question of Rahit observance

---

[19] W. H. McLeod, 'Ahluwalias and Ramgarhias: Two Sikh Castes', *South Asia*, 4 (Oct. 1974), 78–90.

[20] 'The absorption of the *sahajdhārī* Sikhs into the Hindu fold adds weight to the argument that there is no such thing as a clean-shaven Sikh. At one time *sahajdhārī* Sikhism was—as the meaning of the word signified, "those-who-take-time"—the halfway house to the hirsute form of Khalsa Sikhism. Now the process is reversed, and it has become a halfway house to Hinduism.' Khushwant Singh, *A History of the Sikhs*, ii (Princeton, 1966), 303.

has lapsed, nor that hair-cutting has ceased to be an issue as far as Sikh identity is concerned. Within the Punjab, tradition may still maintain a strong hold, but this certainly is not the case overseas. Although no one can offer actual statistics, the usual impression is that in England and North America a substantial majority of Sikhs cut their hair. The crisis of the middle and late 1980s has done something to slow the trend, but it still continues and it will presumably gather speed again when peace returns to the Punjab.

The trend is a predictable one because pressures to conform to the Khalsa ideal (which are usually very strong in the Punjab) are actually reversed in Western societies. Theoretically neutral on such issues, Western societies actually offer firm encouragement to remove the alien turban. A beard can be retained, but a Western-style beard with trimmed hair certainly does not qualify as an acceptable version of the Kes-dhari mode. For second-generation diaspora Sikhs the pressures can be even stronger, particularly for boys wearing turbans at school.

Are these clean-shaven or trimmed Sikhs of Southall and Toronto still Sikhs? It seems that the pragmatic answer largely depends on the individual's antecedents or on continuing contact with the gurdwara. Those who belong to families with a Khalsa tradition will still be regarded as Sikhs, a status which is normally signalled by retention of the names Singh and Kaur. This, in practice, includes all Jats. For others more will depend on the second criterion and if they maintain an association with a gurdwara few will question their right to regard themselves as Sikhs.

For overseas Sikhs this condition may prove to be a temporary one. The pressure to which they expose themselves in Western countries can be very powerful and these pressures will certainly encourage a dissolution of the traditional identity over the course of two or three generations (perhaps less). If this were to occur, there would be a general abandoning of Khalsa symbols accompanied by a continued yet diminishing loyalty to the gurdwara. It is, however, far from certain that any such collapse will occur overseas and it is inconceivable that it could happen in the Punjab. What is certain is that many who claim to be Sikhs will continue to cut their hair, leaving us with the problem of how to frame a definition which accommodates both the strict Khalsa and those who in practice set aside the Rahit.

We should clearly understand that those who set aside the Rahit in such circumstances are not adopting a Sahaj-dhari identity. As we have already noted, the term Sahaj-dhari properly applies to a small and rapidly dwindling remnant comprising those who have never accepted

the Khalsa tradition. We speak now of those who retain a Khalsa affiliation and if we must find a label to distinguish them from the Kes-dhari
Sikh the only one available appears to be Mona. It is, however, in-
sufficiently precise for our purposes and it may one day be necessary to
find a narrower substitute. The word *monā* means 'shaven' and it has
been commonly used in the past to designate any Sikh who cuts his hair.
As such it serves as the antonym to Kes-dhari, a broad term which
incorporates the specific Sahaj-dhari identity. Because the Sahaj-dhari
identity still sustains a fragile existence, it must be retained within any
schema which may be devised. This means that we still lack a term which
designates a Sikh who cuts his hair yet retains a Khalsa affiliation.

The pattern which emerges from this unsatisfactory state of affairs is
represented in fig. 1. There are actually two terms missing from this

Khalsa	Affiliated Khalsa	Non-Khalsa
K e s - d h a r i	M o n a	
Amrit-dhari		Sahaj-dhari

Fig. 1.

diagram, both of them within the 'Affiliated Khalsa' category and
together occupying the whole of that category. Just as we lack a term to
designate the hair-cutting Khalsa affiliate, so too do we lack one which
will distinguish the Kes-dhari who has not become an Amrit-dhari (see
fig. 2). All Amrit-dharis are Kes-dharis, but most Kes-dharis are not
Amrit-dharis. Similarly, all Sahaj-dharis are Monas but most Monas are
not Sahaj-dharis. All will claim to be Sikhs and if their claims are to be
respected an all-inclusive definition will have to be devised.

Khalsa	Affiliated Khalsa	Non-Khalsa
K e s - d h a r i	M o n a	
Amrit-dhari	? ?	Sahaj-dhari

Fig. 2.

One other uncertainty indicated by the diagram concerns the Patit
Sikh. We have already noted that the Patit Sikh is one who has violated
the Khalsa vow and that strictly speaking the term can only be applied to
lapsed Amrit-dharis. A part of the uncertainty arises from the fact that it
is frequently attached to any Kes-dhari who smokes or cuts his hair, not

merely to the formally initiated Amrit-dhari.[21] The other aspect concerns the actual status of the Patit following his lapse. He (or she) must certainly be removed from the Khalsa category, but is the perceived destination to be 'Non-Khalsa' or 'Affiliated Khalsa'? (see fig. 3)

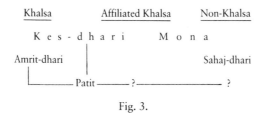

Fig. 3.

A strict answer would probably demand the former. A pragmatic answer would almost certainly indicate the latter.

One final question should be briefly considered before we attempt to draw these scattered items into a single definition. Certain sectarian groups (notably the Nirankaris and Namdharis) claim to be Sikh. Are these claims accepted?

It seems to be generally agreed within the Panth that acceptance should be withheld in the case of any group which draws a substantial body of support from Hindu society or adopts practices which orthodox Sikhs find offensive. Are the Nirankaris and Namdharis thereby excluded? What of the numerous other movements of which prominent examples are provided by the Radhasoami Satsang or the Sikh Dharma of the Western hemisphere? Should all sects be excluded or are there some which most Khalsa Sikhs will own as members of the Panth?

The Nirankaris, like the Namdharis, have been treated briefly above.[22] It is important to distinguish the Nirankaris (the so-called Asali Nirankaris or 'True Nirankaris') from the Sant Nirankaris, the sect whose bitter dispute with Sikhs of the Khalsa played such a prominent part in the events leading up to the storming of the Golden Temple complex in June 1984. The Asali Nirankaris, as we noted before, trace their beginnings to Baba Dayal (1783–1855), who endeavoured to reclaim the Sikhs of the Rawalpindi area from the temptations associated with military triumph under Maharaja Ranjit Singh. Sikhs were, he believed, increasingly

[21] The 1958 draft bill proposing improvements in the administration of gurdwaras included the following definition of a Patit Sikh: '"Patit" means a person who being a Keshadhari Sikh trims or shaves his beard or keshas or who after taking amrit commits any or more of the four kurahits.' *All India Sikh Gurdwaras Legislation* (Amritsar, 1958), 30.

[22] See above, pp. 63–65.

neglecting their duty to remember Akal Purakh through the practice of *nām simaraṇ*. His duty was therefore to preach the message of liberation through the *nām* and to insist upon *nām simaraṇ* as the one effective means. In 1947 the Nirankaris abandoned their centre in Rawalpindi and established themselves on the Indian side of the border in Chandigarh from where their activities are administered to the present day.

The stress which the Nirankaris lay upon *nām simaraṇ* certainly does not qualify them to be regarded as heretics, nor does the outward appearance of the community (whose members include both Amrit-dhari and Sahaj-dhari Sikhs) or reverence for the scripture. Their one fault in the eyes of the orthodox Khalsa lies in their acknowledgement of a continuing line of Gurus descending from Baba Dayal. In this respect the Nirankaris do not question the historic line of Gurus from Nanak to Gobind Singh, nor do they claim any connection with it beyond the beliefs which they share with all Sikhs. Baba Dayal preached renewal and it is for constant renewal in their Sikh faith that the adherents of the movement maintain their faith in the line of Gurus which descends from him.[23]

Confronted by this doctrine, an orthodox Sikh of the Khalsa would have to conclude that the Nirankaris were strictly heretical and some might well have difficulty in regarding them as fellow Sikhs. Such patent heresy is, however, accompanied by a conspicuous dedication to other features of the Sikh tradition and many more would give them the benefit of the doubt. Teja Singh was clearly speaking for the Singh Sabha when he declared that the differences were 'already obliterated almost completely'.[24]

Although the major emphasis of the Namdharis or Kuka Sikhs differs from that of the Nirankaris (a purified Khalsa as opposed to the Nanak-panthi professions of the Nirankaris), the same conclusion must also apply to them. Their origins were very similar to those of the Nirankaris apart from the caste membership of the predominant group.[25] From Hazro and the Peshawar region Baba Balak Singh (1797–1862) also preached the doctrine of *nām simaraṇ* as a remedy for the ills of Maharaja Ranjit Singh's time. He was succeeded by the most famous of all Namdhari Gurus, Baba Ram Singh (1816–85), who stressed the paramount need for a restored Khalsa and who moved the centre of the

[23] John C. B. Webster, *The Nirankari Sikhs* (Delhi, 1979), 9–11, 39–43. McLeod (trans.), *Textual Sources for the Study of Sikhism*, pp. 121–4.

[24] Teja Singh, *Sikhism: Its Ideals and Institutions* (rev. edn., Bombay, 1951), 71.

[25] The Nirankaris were principally Khatris and Aroras. The Namdharis, particularly under Ram Singh and his successors, were drawn mainly from the Ramgarhias and poorer Jats.

group's activities down the Punjab to Bhaini Raian in Ludhiana District. From there (with an important second centre at Sirsa in Haryana) the movement still continues to function.[26]

The Namdharis are more overtly heretical than the Nirankaris as they claim that their line of Gurus continues without break the sequence begun by Guru Nanak. (Guru Gobind Singh, they believe, lived his later life in secret as Baba Ajapal Singh until he 'departed for his heavenly abode' at the age of 146 in 1812.) Namdhari men also differ from ordinary Sikhs as they always wear white homespun clothing and tie their turbans horizontally across the forehead.[27] Their loyalty to the traditions of the Khalsa as they understand them is altogether too obvious to be ignored and only the strictly orthodox would be prepared to place them outside the circle of Sikhs. Faced by their devotion, the Singh Sabha in general and Teja Singh in particular concluded that, even if they were astray on one vital point, they were at least potentially aligned with the Panth.[28] Ganda Singh declares the story of Ajapal Singh to be 'pure fiction of recent creation',[29] but does little else to dispute the claims of the Namdharis to be regarded as Sikhs.

The battles over Nirankari and Namdhari membership were fought many years ago and the issue in their case has been reluctantly conceded. It is not so evidently conceded in the case of the Radhasoami Satsang of Beas, a movement which the Panth is finding much more difficult to digest. The comparatively recent origins of the Beas Satsang are only a part of the problem, for if this were the only objection it would be possible to treat it as the following of a Sant. A more serious objection (particularly in these days of heightened intercommunal tension) is the nature of their teachings and the substantial Hindu membership of the Satsang. If there is a place for Hindus in the Radhasoami Satsang of Beas, its doctrines will be regarded by a Khalsa Sikh at least with considerable suspicion and probably with outright condemnation.

The Radhasoami Satsang is a Sant movement which traces its origins to its foundation in Agra by Swami Shiv Dayal in 1861. During the movement's second generation the two principal disciples of Shiv Dayal organized separate branches, one of them on the banks of the Beas River

---

[26] Fauja Singh Bajwa, *Kuka Movement* (Delhi, 1965). W. H. McLeod, 'The Kukas: A Millenarian Sect of the Punjab', in G. A. Wood and P. S. O'Connor (eds.), *W. P. Morrell: A tribute* (Dunedin, 1973), 85–103.

[27] McLeod (trans.), *Textual Sources for the Study of Sikhism*, pp. 126–7.

[28] Teja Singh, *Sikhism: Its Ideals and Institutions*, p. 71.

[29] Ganda Singh, *Guru Gobind Singh's Death at Nanded: An Examination of Succession Theories* (Faridkot, 1972), 78.

in Amritsar District. This was the group led by Jaimal Singh, who in 1903 was succeeded by Sawan Singh or 'the Great Master'. A line of Gurus was thereby established, teaching the threefold message of *simaraṇ* (by which is meant repetition of the Lord's many Names until attention is focused on the Third Eye which lies within), *dhyān* (contemplation of the immortal form of the Master), and *bhajan* (listening to the celestial music within us).[30]

Not surprisingly the Satsang attracted many Hindus, adding to the offence which it caused by acknowledging a succession of Gurus. Equally unsurprising is the difficulty which most Khalsa Sikhs have in accommodating its teachings within the Panth, with the result that its Sikh members are viewed as marginal to say the least. What then do Khalsa Sikhs make of Sikh Dharma of the Western hemisphere, founded by its present leader Harbhajan Singh Khalsa Yogiji (or Yogi Bhajan)? This group, commonly known by the title of its educational branch as 3HO (Healthy Happy Holy Organization), was founded in the United States by Yogi Bhajan in 1971 and is thus a comparatively recent movement. Its members wear white apparel (including turbans for women as well as for men) and lead a rigorous life of yoga and meditation. The style of yoga practised by the group is called Kundalini Yoga and, although a successor to Yogi Bhajan has not yet been appointed, it is assumed that he will be followed by one of his disciples. An ordained ministry is also a distinctive feature of the movement.[31]

Sikhs who come in contact with Sikh Dharma are frequently perplexed by it, not knowing whether to embrace its followers as unusually devout or to avoid them as perversely unorthodox. To those nurtured on Guru Nanak's conflict with the Nath yogis, Kundalini Yoga seems distinctly suspicious and the enthusiasm of Yogi Bhajan's youthful followers makes them uneasy, particularly when it favours moral absolutes over

[30] Mark Juergensmeyer, 'The Radhasoami revival of the Sant Tradition', in Karine Schomer and W. H. McLeod (eds.), *The Sants: Studies in a Devotional Tradition of India* (Berkeley and Delhi, 1987), 331–5. The Beas Satsang has split several times. When Sawan Singh passed the succession on to Jagat Singh, a disappointed contender, Kirpal Singh, moved to Delhi and there founded the Ruhani Satsang. The family members of Maharajji, the boy guru at the centre of the Divine Light Mission, were also followers of the Beas Satsang. The American movement known as Eckankar was founded by Paul Twitchell, an initiate of Kirpal Singh. Ibid. 334–5.
[31] See the various articles by Verne A. Dusenbery, for example his 'Punjabi Sikhs and *Gorā* Sikhs: Conflicting Assertions of Sikh Identity in North America', in R. H. Brown *et al.* (eds.), *Tradition and Transformation: Essays on Migration and the Indian Diaspora* (New Delhi, forthcoming); and 'The Sikh Person, the Khalsa Panth and Western Sikh Converts', in Jayant K. Lele *et al.* (eds.), *Boeings and Bullock-carts: Rethinking India's Restructuring* (Leiden, forthcoming).

Punjabi notions of honour (*izzat*). But then the obedience of 3HO Sikhs to panthic ideals seems highly commendable and their loyalty to Khalsa observance appears to be beyond question. The answer appears to be to let them live their life of obedience, and Punjabis will live another, seldom the twain meeting in any meaningful way. They are accepted as Sikhs provided they maintain a separate existence.

The last of these groups to be noted produces an entirely different reaction. The Sant Nirankari Mandal elicits condemnation of the most violent kind, sufficient to ensure that no Sikh of the Khalsa will ever be a follower. Its foundation, although difficult to ascertain, probably occurred in the years immediately before Partition in 1947. Baba Buta Singh, often identified as the founder, was a member of the Nirankari Darbar who during the 1930s was asked to stay away from meetings of the Darbar until he had brought his drinking under control. In 1943 he died, still a Nirankari. He had, however, a group of followers and one of these, Baba Avtar Singh, seems to have been responsible for the break-away in the years following Buta Singh's death.[32] Frequently, to the inexpressible dismay of the old Nirankari Darbar, the two groups are confused and the term Nirankari incorrectly used when the Sant Nirankaris are intended. By those who understand the difference, the Sant Nirankaris are commonly styled the Nakali Nirankaris (the 'Spurious Nirankaris') as opposed to the older Asali Nirankaris.

The principal differences are said to be the inclusion of other works together with the Adi Granth in the scriptures venerated by the Sant Nirankaris, together with the exalted homage which they pay to their leader as Guru. This, however, does not explain the depth of orthodox feeling towards them. For several years prior to 1978 relations between the Sant Nirankari Mandal and the Akali Dal, never cordial, had been deteriorating still further. On 13 April of that year there occurred a demonstration against a Sant Nirankari conference in Amritsar and the fatal police shooting. This was the event which thrust Jarnail Singh Bhindranwale to the forefront of public notice, for he was the leader of the protesters. His violent denunciations of the Sant Nirankaris were widely reported and in 1980 their leader, Baba Gurbachan Singh, was assassinated.[33] No Sikh of the Khalsa could possibly contemplate membership of the Sant Nirankari Mandal. Whoever a Sikh might be, he would not be Sant Nirankari.

---

[32] Webster, *The Nirankari Sikhs*, pp. 34–5.
[33] Khushwant Singh, 'The Genesis', in Abida Samiuddin (ed.), *The Punjab Crisis: Challenge and Response*, (Delhi, 1985), 96–7.

As one would expect, therefore, Khalsa attitudes towards sectarian movements are ambivalent. The Asali Nirankaris and the Namdharis are held by most to be Sikhs, a view which the strict might question but most would probably concede. Yogi Bhajan and his followers seem to attract a similar verdict, disputed by some yet grudgingly acknowledged by many more. The Radhasoamis, with all their offshoots, are distinctly marginal; and adherents of the Sant Nirankari Mandal are vehemently excluded.

We shall now attempt to draw these various items into a summary statement and we begin with what a Sikh is not. It seems clear that a very substantial majority of Sikhs now reject the claim that Sikhs are Hindus or that the Panth is a Hindu sect. The Panth's origins were Hindu and its partial retention of caste must be acknowledged, but the experiences and responses of the past five centuries have together generated a sense of separate identity. A few Sikhs may still regard themselves as Hindus. Most do not.

How then is their distinctive identity to be defined? By this time ample warning has been issued concerning the problems involved in this enterprise. The attempt must nevertheless be made, regardless of the certainty that its result will be subjected to a wide variety of criticisms. The following definition is offered on the basis of the foregoing interpretation.

A Sikh is a person who reveres the ten Gurus (the lineage which begins with Guru Nanak and concludes with Guru Gobind Singh). The teachings of Guru Nanak and his successors concerning liberation through the divine Name are incorporated in the scripture known as the Adi Granth. Although some Sikhs may not be aware of the contents of this scripture, all will certainly venerate the scripture itself. They will also acknowledge the practice of *nām simaran* to be mandatory, though for many the acknowledgement may be implicit and the actual practice rudimentary. The building or room which ritually houses the Adi Granth is called a gurdwara and all Sikhs acknowledge the sanctity which the scripture confers on it. They also recognize the role of the gurdwara in expressing the anti-caste ideals of the Gurus.

Those who acknowledge allegiance to Guru Nanak and his successors constitute the community originally known as the Nanakpanth and now called simply the Panth. During the time of Guru Gobind Singh, members of the Panth were summoned to accept initiation into the Khalsa order and thereafter to observe its code of discipline (the Rahit). Prominent amongst the many features of the Rahit are a group of distinctive Sikh rituals and a series of personal obligations which include the Five Ks. Two particularly conspicuous items are the prohibition of hair-cutting and a rigorous ban on smoking. It is believed that shortly before his death Guru Gobind Singh declared the line of personal Gurus to be at an end. Thereafter the authority of the Guru was to be vested in the Adi Granth (the Guru Granth) and the corporate community (the Guru Panth).

All orthodox Sikhs accept these statements as the authentic commandments of Guru Gobind Singh and, although they may not actually undergo initiation, they will at least observe the basic requirements of the Rahit. These may be defined in practical terms as a scrupulous observance of the bans on hair-cutting and smoking. Those who decline to accept the basic requirements of the Rahit can still be accepted as Sikhs, but only on the understanding that they are failing to discharge customary duties.

Sikhs are heirs to a history and a fund of tradition which they should regard as a continuing source of guidance and inspiration. Although the basic principles of the Panth include a denial of caste, the continuation of caste practices is nevertheless recognized as unavoidable, and those who observe such practices are not thereby deprived of their right to be regarded as Sikhs.

Within the Panth women enjoy a status which theoretically is equal to that of male Sikhs. Although most Sikhs are Punjabis, the Panth is open to any who accept its doctrines and practice.

It must surely be obvious that in the framing of this summary definition historical corners have been cut and that the word 'orthodox' has been used to cover what should properly be treated as an assumption rather than as a proven fact. The only possible defence is that complex communities can never be summarized in neat, concise, unqualified terms. In the end, however, the attempt must be made. Time and the response of others will decide its success.

SELECT BIBLIOGRAPHY

ENGLISH

ABIDA SAMIUDDIN (ed.), *The Punjab Crisis: Challenge and Response* (Delhi, 1985).

AMARJIT SINGH SETHI, *Universal Sikhism* (New Delhi, 1972).

AMRIK SINGH (ed.), *Punjab in Indian Politics: Issues and Trends* (Delhi, 1985).

ANUP CHAND KAPUR, *The Punjab Crisis: An Analytical Study* (New Delhi, 1985).

ATTAR SINGH, *Secularism and the Sikh Faith* (Amritsar, 1973).

ATTAR SINGH OF BHADAUR (trans.), *The Rayhit Nama of Pralad Rai or the Excellent Conversation of Duswan Padsha, and Nand Lal's Rayhit Nama or Rules for the Guidance of Sikhs in Religious Matters* (Lahore, 1876).

—— *The Sakhee Book, or the Description of Gooroo Gobind Singh's Religion and Doctrines* (Benares, 1873).

—— *Travels of Guru Tegh Bahadur and Gobind Singh* (Allahabad, 1876).

AVTAR SINGH, *Ethics of the Sikhs* (Patiala, 1970).

BALDEV RAJ NAYAR, *Minority Politics in the Punjab* (Princeton, 1966).

BALWANT SINGH ANAND, *Guru Nanak: His Life was his Message* (New Delhi, 1983).

—— *Guru Nanak: Religion and Ethics* (Patiala, 1968).

BANERJEE A. C., *Guru Nanak and his Times* (Patiala, 1971).

—— *Guru Nanak to Guru Gobind Singh* (New Delhi, 1978).

—— *The Khalsa Raj* (New Delhi, 1985).

BARRIER, N. GERALD, *The Sikhs and their Literature* (Delhi, 1970).

—— and DUSENBERY, VERNE A., *Aspects of Modern Sikhism* (Michigan Papers on Sikh Studies, No. 1; 1985).

—— and WALLACE PAUL, *The Punjab Press, 1880–1905* (East Lansing, 1970).

BEDI, K. S., and BAL, S. S. (eds.), *Essays on History, Literature, Art and Culture Presented to Dr M. S. Randhawa* (New Delhi, 1970).

BHAGAT SINGH, *Sikh Polity in the Eighteenth and Nineteenth Centuries* (New Delhi, 1978).

BHUSHAN CHANDER BHALLA, *The Punjab belongs to the Sikhs* (Lahore, 1947).

BIKRAMA JIT HASRAT, *Life and Times of Ranjit Singh* (Nabha, 1977).

BINGLEY, A. H., *History, Caste and Culture of Jats and Gujars* (1899; 2nd edn., New Delhi, 1978).

—— *Sikhs* (Simla, 1899).

BRASS, PAUL R., *Language, Religion, and Politics in North India* (Cambridge, 1974).

COLE, W. OWEN, *The Guru in Sikhism* (London, 1982).

—— *Sikhism and its Indian Context, 1469–1708* (London, 1984).

—— and PIARA SINGH SAMBHI, *The Sikhs: Their Religious Beliefs and Practices* (London, 1978).

COURT, H. (trans.), *History of the Sikhs* (Lahore, 1888).

CROOKE, W., *The Popular Religion and Folk-lore of Northern India* (Westminster, 1896).

CUNNINGHAM, J. D., *A History of the Sikhs* (1st edn., London, 1849; rev. edn. Oxford, 1918).

DALIP SINGH, *Dynamics of Punjab Politics* (New Delhi, 1981).

DALJEET SINGH, *The Sikh Ideology* (New Delhi, 1984).

—— *Sikhism: A Comparative Study of its Theology and Mysticism* (New Delhi, 1979).

DARSHAN SINGH, *Indian Bhakti Tradition and Sikh Gurus* (Chandigarh, 1968).

DATTA, V. N., *Amritsar Past and Present* (Amritsar, 1967).

DHARAM PAL ASHTA, *The Poetry of the Dasam Granth* (New Delhi, 1959).

ELLIOT, H. M., *Memoirs on the History, Folk-lore, and Distribution of the Races of the North Western Provinces of India* (2 vols.; London, 1869).

FALCON, R. W., *Handbook on Sikhs for the Use of Regimental Officers* (Allahabad, 1896).

FAUJA SINGH, *After Ranjit Singh* (New Delhi, 1982).

—— *Guru Amar Das: Life and Teachings* (New Delhi, 1979).

—— (ed.), *The City of Amritsar: A Study of Historical, Cultural, Social and Economic Aspects* (New Delhi, 1978).

—— (ed.), *Papers on Guru Nanak* (Patiala, 1969).

—— and ARORA, A. C. (eds.), *Maharaja Ranjit Singh: Politics, Society and Economy* (Patiala, 1984).

—— and GURBACHAN SINGH TALIB, *Guru Tegh Bahadur: Martyr and Teacher* (Patiala, 1975).

—— *et al.*, *Sikhism* (Patiala, 1979).

FAUJA SINGH BAJWA, *Kuka Movement* (Delhi, 1965).

FORSTER, GEORGE D., *A Journey from Bengal to England* (London, 1798).

FOX, RICHARD G., *Lions of the Punjab: Culture in the Making* (Berkeley and Los Angeles, 1985).

GANDA SINGH, *Ahmad Shah Durrani* (Bombay, 1959).

—— *Banda Singh Bahadur* (Amritsar, 1935).

—— (ed.), *Bhagat Lakshman Singh: Autobiography* (Calcutta, 1965).

—— (ed.), *Early European Accounts of the Sikhs* (Calcutta, 1962).

—— (trans.), *Nanak Panthis, or the Sikhs and Sikhism of the 17th century*, Eng. trans. of a chapter from Muhsin Fani, *Dabistān-i-Mazāhib* (Madras, 1939).

—— (ed.), *Sources of the Life and Teachings of Guru Nanak* (Patiala, 1969).

GOBIND SINGH MANSUKHANI, *Aspects of Sikhism* (New Delhi, 1982).

GOBINDER SINGH, *Religion and Politics in the Punjab* (New Delhi, 1986).

GOKUL CHAND NARANG, *Transformation of Sikhism* (1st edn., Lahore, 1914; rev. edn., Lahore, 1946).

GOPAL SINGH, *A History of the Sikh People, 1469–1978* (New Delhi, 1979).

GREWAL, J. S., *From Guru Nanak to Maharaja Ranjit Singh: Essays in Sikh History* (Amritsar, 1972).

—— *Guru Nanak in History* (Chandigarh, 1969).

—— *Miscellaneous Articles* (Amritsar, 1974).

—— *The Reign of Maharaja Ranjit Singh* (Patiala, 1981).

—— *The Sikhs of the Punjab* (Cambridge, forthcoming).

—— and BAL, S. S., *Guru Gobind Singh: A Biographical Study* (Chandigarh, 1978).

—— and INDU BANGA (eds.), *Maharaja Ranjit Singh and his Times* (Amritsar, 1980).

GURBACHAN SINGH TALIB, *Guru Nanak: His Personality and Vision* (Delhi, 1969).

GURDEV SINGH (ed.), *Perspectives on the Sikh Tradition* (Patiala, 1986).

GURMUKH NIHAL SINGH, *Guru Nanak: His Life, Time and Teaching* (Delhi, 1969).

HARBANS SINGH, *Bhai Vir Singh* (New Delhi, 1972).

—— *Guru Gobind Singh* (Chandigarh, 1966; 2nd rev. edn., New Delhi, 1979).

—— *Guru Nanak and the Origins of the Sikh Faith* (Bombay, 1969).

—— *Guru Tegh Bahadur* (New Delhi, 1982).

—— *The Heritage of the Sikhs* (Bombay, 1964; 2nd rev. edn., New Delhi, 1983).

—— and BARRIER, N. GERALD (eds.), *Punjab Past and Present: Essays in Honour of Dr Ganda Singh* (Patiala, 1976).

HARI RAM GUPTA, *History of the Sikhs* (3rd rev. edn.; 8 vols.; New Delhi, 1978–88).

HARJOT SINGH OBEROI, 'A World Reconstructed: Religion, Ritual and Community among the Sikhs, 1850–1909', unpub. Ph.D. thesis (Australian National University, Canberra, 1987).

HERSHMAN, PAUL, *Punjabi Kinship and Marriage* (Delhi, 1981).

IBBETSON, D., *Outlines of Panjab Ethnography* (Calcutta, 1883).

—— *Panjab Castes* (Lahore, 1916).

INDUBHUSAN BANERJEE, *Evolution of the Khalsa* (2 vols.; Calcutta, 1936).

JAGJIT SINGH, *Perspectives on Sikh Studies* (New Delhi, 1985).

—— *The Sikh Revolution* (New Delhi, 1981).

JAYANT K. LELE *et al.* (eds.), *Boeings and Bullock-carts: Rethinking India's restructuring* (Leiden, forthcoming).

JEFFRY, ROBIN, *What's Happening to India?* (London, 1986).

JITINDER KAUR, *The Politics of Sikhs: A Study of Delhi Sikh Gurdwara Management Committee* (New Delhi, 1986).

JODH SINGH, *Some Studies in Sikhism* (Ludhiana, 1953).

JOGENDRA SINGH (comp.), *Sikh Ceremonies* (Bombay, 1941).

JUERGENSMEYER, M., and BARRIER, N. GERALD (eds.), *Sikh Studies: Comparative Perspectives on a Changing Tradition* (Berkeley, 1979).

KAILASH CHANDER GULATI, *The Akalis Past and Present* (New Delhi, 1974).

KANWALJIT KAUR and INDARJIT SINGH (trans.), *Rehat Maryada: A Guide to the Sikh Way of Life* (London, 1971).

KAPUR SINGH, *Parasharprasna, or the Baisakhi of Guru Gobind Singh* (Jullundur, 1959).

KHAZAN SINGH, *History and Philosophy of the Sikh Religion* (2 vols.; Lahore, 1914).

KHUSHWANT SINGH, *A History of the Sikhs* (2 vols.; Princeton, 1963, 1966).

KULDIP NAYAR and KHUSHWANT SINGH, *Tragedy of Punjab: Operation Bluestar and after* (New Delhi, 1984).

LAKSHMAN SINGH, *Sikh Martyrs* (Madras, 1923).

LOEHLIN, C. H., *The Granth of Guru Gobind Singh and the Khalsa Brotherhood* (Lucknow, 1971).

—— *The Sikhs and their Scriptures* (Lucknow, 1958).

MACAULIFFE, M. A., *The Sikh Religion: Its Gurus, Sacred Writings and Authors* (6 vols. in 3; Oxford, 1909).

McLEOD, W. H. (trans.), *The B40 Janam-sākhī* (Amritsar, 1980).

—— (trans.), *The Chaupā Siṅgh Rahit-nāmā* (Dunedin, 1987).

—— *Early Sikh Tradition: A Study of the Janam-sākhīs* (Oxford, 1980).

—— *The Evolution of the Sikh Community* (Oxford, 1976).

—— *Gurū Nānak and the Sikh Religion* (Oxford, 1968; 2nd edn., Delhi, 1976).

—— *The Sikhs: History, Religion and Society* (New York, 1989).

—— (trans.), *Textual Sources for the Study of Sikhism* (Manchester, 1984).

MADANJIT KAUR, *The Golden Temple Past and Present* (Amritsar, 1983).

MALCOLM, JOHN, 'Sketch of the Sikhs', *Asiatick Researches*, xi (Calcutta, 1810); republished as *Sketch of the Sikhs* (London, 1812).

MARENCO, ETHNE K., *The Transformation of Sikh Society* (Portland, 1974).

MEHAR SINGH CHADDAH, *Are Sikhs a Nation?* (Delhi, 1982).

MOHINDER SINGH, *The Akali Movement* (Delhi, 1978).

MUKHERJEE, S. N. (ed), *India: History and Thought* (Calcutta, 1982).

NARANG, A. S., *Storm over the Sutlej: The Akali Politics* (New Delhi, 1983).

NARENDRA KRISHNA SINHA, *Ranjit Singh* (Calcutta, 1951).

—— *Rise Of the Sikh Power* (Calcutta, 1946).

NIHARRANJAN RAY, *The Sikh Gurus and the Sikh Society* (Patiala, 1970).

O'CONNELL, JOSEPH D. *et al.* (eds.), *Sikh History and Religion in the Twentieth Century* (Toronto, 1988).

PARKASH SINGH, *The Sikh Gurus and the Temple of Bread* (Amritsar, 1964).

PETRIE, D., 'Secret C.I.D. Memorandum on Recent Developments in Sikh Politics', dated 11 August 1911, *The Panjab Past and Present*, 4/2 (Oct. 1970), 300–79.

PETTIGREW, JOYCE, *Robber Noblemen: A Study of the Political System of the Sikh Jats* (London, 1975).

PRINSEP, H. T., *Origin of the Sikh Power in the Punjab and the Political Life of Muharaja Runjeet Singh* (Calcutta, 1834).

PURAN SINGH, *The Book of the Ten Masters* (London, 1926).

RAJIV A. KAPUR, *Sikh Separatism: The Politics of Faith* (London, 1986).

RAVINDER G. B. SINGH, *Indian Philosophical Tradition and Guru Nanak* (Patiala, 1983).

Rehat Maryada: A Guide to the Sikh Way of Life (Amritsar, 1978).

ROSE, H. A. (ed.), *A Glossary of the Tribes and Castes of the Punjab and North-West Frontier Province* (3 vols.; Lahore, 1911–19).

RUCHI RAM SAHNI, *Struggle for Reform in Sikh Shrines* (Amritsar, 1964).

SAHIB SINGH, *Guru Nanak Dev and his Teachings* (Jullundur, 1969).

SANTOKH SINGH, *Philosophical Foundations of the Sikh Value System* (New Delhi, 1982).

SARDUL SINGH CAVEESHAR, *The Sikh Studies* (Lahore, 1937).

SCHOMER, KARINE, and MCLEOD, W. H. (eds.), *The Sants: Studies in a Devotional Tradition of India* (Berkeley and Delhi, 1987).

SHACKLE, C., *The Sikhs* (London, 1984; rev. edn., 1986).

SHER SINGH GYANI, *Philosophy of Sikhism* (Lahore, 1944).

Sikhism and Indian Society (Transactions of the Indian Institute of Advanced Study, 4; Simla, 1967).

SURINDAR SINGH KOHLI, *A Critical Study of Adi Granth* (New Delhi, 1961).

—— *Sikh Ethics* (New Delhi, 1975).

SURINDER SINGH JOHAR, *Handbook on Sikhism* (Delhi, 1977).

—— *The Heritage of Amritsar* (Delhi, 1978).

SURJIT SINGH GANDHI, *History of the Sikh Gurus* (Delhi, 1978).

—— *The Struggle of the Sikhs for Sovereignty* (Delhi, 1980).

SURJIT SINGH HANS, 'Historical analysis of Sikh literature, A.D. 1500–1850', unpub. Ph.D. thesis (Guru Nanak Dev University, Amritsar, 1980).

TARAN SINGH (ed.), *Sikh Gurus and the Indian Spiritual Thought* (Patiala, 1981).

TEJA SINGH, *Essays in Sikhism* (Lahore, 1944).

—— *The Gurdwara Reform Movement and the Sikh Awakening* (Jullundur, 1922; 2nd edn., Amritsar, 1984).

—— *Sikhism: Its Ideals and Institutions* (1938; rev. edn., Calcutta, 1951).

—— and GANDA SINGH, *A Short History of the Sikhs* (Bombay, 1950).

The Sikh Religion: A Symposium by M. Macauliffe, H. H. Wilson, F. Pincott, J. Malcolm, and Sardar Kahan Singh (Calcutta, 1958).

TRILOCHAN SINGH, *Guru Tegh Bahadur: Prophet and Martyr* (Delhi, 1967).

—— *The Turban and the Sword of the Sikhs* (Gravesend, 1977).

TUTEJA, K. L., *Sikh Politics (1920–40)* (Kurukshetra, 1984).

WALLACE, PAUL, and SURENDRA CHOPRA (eds.), *Political Dynamics of the Punjab* (Amritsar, 1981; 2nd edn., forthcoming).

WEBSTER, JOHN C. B., *The Nirankari Sikhs* (Delhi, 1979).

PUNJABI

ABNAS KAUR, *Bhāī Mohan Singh Vaid dī vārtak vanagī* (Patiala, 1976).

AMAR SINGH, *Singh Sabhā lahir de ughe sānchālak Giānī Dit Singh Jī* (Amritsar, 1962).

AVTAR SINGH, *Khālsā dharam śāstar* (Anandpur, 1914).

BHAGAT SINGH, *Giānī Giān Singh* (Patiala, 1978).

DALIP SINGH 'Dip', *Gurū Amar Dās* (Patiala, 1980).

DALJIT SINGH, *Singh Sabhā de moḍhī Bhāī Dit Singh Jī* (Amritsar, 1951).

DIT SINGH, *Guramati ārtī prabodh* (Lahore, 1900).

—— *Gurū Nānak prabodh* (Lahore, 1890).

—— *Kalgīdhar upkār* (Lahore, 1899).

—— *Nakalī Sikh prabodh* (Lahore, 1895).

—— *Pammā prabodh* (Lahore, 1906).

GANDA SINGH (samp.), *Pañjāb (1849–1960): Bhāī Jodh Singh abhinandan granth* (Patiala, 1962).

GIAN SINGH, *Srī Gurū Panth Prakāś* (Delhi, 1870; rev. edn., Amritsar, 1923).

—— *Tavarīkh Gurū Khālsā* (2nd edn., Patiala, 1970).

GOBIND SINGH MANSUKHANI, *Gurasikh kī hai?* (Amritsar, 1979).

GURBACHAN SINGH NAIAR (samp.), *Gur ratan māl arathāt sau sākhī* (Patiala, 1985).

GURBAKHSH SINGH, *Merī jīvan kahānī* (2 vols.; Prit Nagar, 1969).

GURDAS BHALLA (Bhai Gurdas), *Vārān Bhāī Gurdās*, samp. Hazara Singh ate Vir Singh (Amritsar, 1962).

Gurmat Prakāś Bhāg Sanskār (Amritsar, 1915).

GURMUKH SINGH, *Sudhārak* (Lahore, 1888).

HARBANS SINGH, *Bhāī Vīr Singh te unhān dī rachanā* (Lahore, 1940).

HARJINDAR SINGH DILGIR, *Sromaṇī Akālī Dal (ik itihās)* (Jalandhar, 1978).

JAGDIS SINGH, *Sāḍe rasam rivāj* (Patiala, 1976).

JAGIR SINGH, *Param Gurū Nānak* (Delhi, 1982).

JAGJIT SINGH, *Ādhunik janam sākhī (jīvan Srī Gurū Nānak Dev Jī)* (Ludhiana, 1970).

—— *Janam-sākhīān Srī Gurū Nānak Dev Jī dā tārkik adhiain* (Ludhiana, 1970).

JIT SINGH SITAL, *Amritsar: siftī dā ghar* (Patiala, 1978).

JODH SINGH, *Guramati niraṇay* (Ludhiana, n.d.).

—— (samp.), *Sikhī kī hai?* (Amritsar, 1911).

KAHN SINGH NABHA (samp.), *Guramat sudhākar* (1st edn., Amritsar, 1901; rev. edn., Patiala, 1970).

—— *Gurumat mārtaṇḍ* (Amritsar, 1962).

—— *Guruśabad ratanākar mahān koś* (1st edn. 4 vols., Patiala, 1931; 2nd edn. 1 vol., Patiala, 1960).

—— *Ham Hindū nahīn* (Amritsar, 1899).

KARAM SINGH, *Itihāsak khoj*, samp. Hira Singh 'Darad' (2nd edn., Amritsar, 1975).

—— *Kattak ki Visākh?* (Amritsar, 1913).

KARTAR SINGH SARHADI, *Singh Sabhā lahir dā sunaharī te mahān praupakarī itihās* (Yamunanagar, 1974).

MAN SINGH NIRANKARI, *Sikh dharam ate sikhī* (Amritsar, 1981).

MUNSHA SINGH DUKHI, *Jīvan Bhāī Sāhib Bhāī Mohan Singh Jī Vaid* (Amritsar, n.d.).

NAND LAL, *Bhāī Nand Lāl granthāvalī*, samp. Ganda Singh (Malacca, 1968).

NARAIN SINGH, *Sikh dharam diān buniādān* (Amritsar, 1966).

PIAR SINGH, *Bhāī Jodh Singh: jīvan te rachanā* (Patiala, 1983).

PIARA SINGH PADAM (samp.), *Rahit-nāme* (Patiala, 1974).

RANDHIR SINGH (samp.), *Prem Sumārg Granth* (1953; 2nd edn., Jalandhar, 1965).

—— *Sikh kaun hai?* (Ludhiana, 1973).

RATAN SINGH BHANGU, *Prāchīn Panth Prakāś*, samp. Vir Singh (Amritsar, 1914; 4th edn., 1962).

RATAN SINGH JAGGI, *Bhāī Gurdās: jīvanī te rachanā* (Patiala, 1974).

—— *Dasam Granth dā kartritav* (New Delhi, 1966).

—— *Dasam Granth dā paurānik adhiain* (Jalandhar, 1965).

—— *Vichār-dhārā* (Patiala, 1966).

S. S. AMOL, *Bhāī Mohan Singh Vaid* (Patiala, 1969).

—— *Profaisar Tejā Singh* (Patiala, 1977).

SAINAPATI, *Kavī Saināpati rachit Srī Gur Sobhā*, samp. Ganda Singh (Patiala, 1967).

SANTOKH SINGH, *Nānak prakāś* and *Sūraj prakāś*, samp. Vir Singh, 13 vols.; i. *Srī Gur pratāp sūraj granthāvalī dī prasāvanā*; ii–iv. *Srī Gur Nānak prakāś*; v–xiii. *Srī Gur pratāp sūraj granth* (Amritsar, 1927–35).

SARDHA RAM, *Sikhān de rāj dī vitthiā* (Lahore, 1892).

SARDUL SINGH, *Sardhā pūran* (Amritsar, 1891).

SATIBIR SINGH, *Sāḍā itihās* (1957; 2nd edn., Jalandhar, 1970).

SEVA SINGH, *Bhāī Mohan Singh Jī Vaid de jīvan de jhalak* (Tarn Taran, 1936).

SHAMSHER SINGH ASHOK, *Pañjāb diān lahirān* (Patiala, 1974).

—— *Prasidh vidvān Bhāī Kāhn Singh Nābhā* (Guara, 1966).

Sikh rahit maryādā (1st edn., Amritsar, 1950).

SOHAN SINGH SITAL (samp.), *Sikh itihās de somen* (5 vols.; Ludhiana, 1981–4).

SUKHJIT KAUR, *Bhāī Kāhn Singh Nābhā te unhān diān rachanāvān* (Patiala, n.d.).

SURAJ SINGH PRACHARAK, *Guramat kāj bivhār* (Lahore, 1913).

SURJIT HANS, *Sikh kī karan?* (Amritsar, 1986).

TEJA SINGH, *Sikh dharam* (Patiala, 1952).

TEJA SINGH OVARASIR, *Khālsā rahit prakāś* (Lahore, 1914).

VIR SINGH, *Srī Aṣṭ Gur chamatakār* (2 vols.; Amritsar, 1952).

—— *Srī Gurū Nānak chamatakār* (2 vols.; Amritsar, 1928–33).

—— *Srī Kalgīdhar chamatakār* (2 vols.; Amritsar, 1925).

GLOSSARY

Ādi Granth: the Guru Granth Sahib, the sacred scripture of the Sikhs compiled by Guru Arjan in 1603–4.

Āhlūwālīā: a Sikh caste of the Punjab, by origin distillers but successful in acquiring a greatly elevated status.

Akālī: follower of Akal Purakh (q.v.); in the eighteenth and early nineteenth centuries a zealous Sikh soldier; in the twentieth century a member of the Akali Dal (Akali Party).

Akāl Purakh: the 'Timeless One', God.

Akāl Takhat: the principal centre of Sikh temporal authority, located immediately adjacent to Darbar Sahib (the Golden Temple).

amrit (amṛta): 'nectar of immortality'; baptismal water used in *amrit sanskār* (q.v.).

Amrit-dhārī: a Sikh who has 'taken *amrit*', viz. an initiated member of the Khalsa (q.v.).

amrit sanskār: the initiation ceremony of the Khalsa. (q.v.).

Anand Kāraj: Sikh marriage ritual.

Ardās: the 'Sikh Prayer', a formal prayer recited at the conclusion of most Sikh rituals.

Aroṛā: a mercantile caste of the Punjab.

Āryā Samāj: Hindu reform movement of the late nineteenth and twentieth centuries (particularly strong in the Punjab), at first sympathetic to the Singh Sabha (q.v.) but soon shifting to hostility.

asalī: true, real.

āsaṇ: mode of sitting adopted by yogis.

Bābā: 'Father', a term of respect applied to holy men.

Baisākhī Day: New Year's Day in India, the first day of the month of Baisakh or Visakh.

bāṇī: works of the Gurus and other poets included in the Sikh sacred scriptures.

bāolī: sacred well.

Bhāī: 'Brother', title of respect.

Bhakta: devotee, one who practises Bhakti (q.v.).

Bhakti: belief in, adoration of a personal god.

chār kurahit: the four gross sins against the Rahit (q.v.) (cutting one's hair, eating meat which has been slaughtered according to the Muslim rite, sexual intercourse with any person other than one's spouse, and using tobacco).

Chief Khalsa Diwan: united body formed in 1902 to conduct the affairs of the Amritsar and Lahore Singh Sabhas (q.v.).

darbār, durbar: court.

darśan: audience; appearance before eminent person, sacred object, etc.

Dasam Granth: the scripture attributed to the authorship or times of Guru Gobind Singh.

dharam (dharma): in Sikh usage the pattern of belief embodied in the Panth; the moral order generally; panthic duty; (modern usage) religion.

dharamsālā: place of worship for early Sikh Panth (later gurdwara, q.v.).

Five Ks: five items (each beginning with the initial 'k') which Sikhs of the Khalsa must wear.

Granth: [the Sacred] Volume, the Adi Granth (q.v.) or Guru Granth Sahib.

granthī: custodian of a gurdwara.

gurbāṇī: works of the Gurus.

gur-bilās: 'splendour of the Guru'; hagiographic narratives of the lives of the Gurus (esp. the sixth and the tenth), stressing their role as warriors.

gurduārā: gurdwara, Sikh temple.

Gurmat: the teachings of the Gurus.

Gursikh: a Sikh of the Khalsa; a punctilious Sikh.

gurū: a spiritual preceptor, either a person or the divine inner voice.

Gurū Granth Sāhib: the Adi Granth (q.v.), specifically in its role as Guru.

Gurū Granth: the Granth in its role as Guru.

Gurū Khālsā: the Khalsa in the role of Guru.

Gurū Panth: the Panth (q.v.) in its role as Guru.

gurumata: 'the intention of the Guru', a resolution passed by the Sarbat Khalsa (q.v.) in the presence of the Guru Granth Sahib.

halāl: flesh of animal killed in accordance with the Muslim ritual whereby it is bled to death (cf. *jhaṭkā*).

Harijan: Outcaste or Scheduled Caste.

haṭha-yoga: the yogic discipline practised by adherents of the Nath tradition (q.v.).

janam-sākhī: traditional narrative of the life of Guru Nanak.

Jaṭ: Punjabi rural caste, numerically dominant in the Panth (q.v.).

jathā: military detachment; touring parties (commonly for singing kirtan or the administration of Khalsa initiation).

jathedār: commander (normally of a jatha).

jhaṭkā: flesh of an animal killed with a single blow, approved for consumption by members of the Khalsa (cf. *halāl*).

kachh: a pair of pants which must not extend below the knees, worn as one of the Five Ks (q.v.).

kaṅghā: wooden comb, worn as one of the Five Ks (q.v.).

Kānphaṭ yogi: 'split-ear' yogi; follower of Gorakhnath, adherent of the Nath tradition (q.v.)

karā: steel bangle, worn as one of the Five Ks (q.v.).

karāh praśād: sacramental food prepared in a large iron dish (*karāhī*).

karma (karam): the destiny, fate of an individual, generated in accordance with the deeds performed in his/her present and past existences.

kathā: homily.

Khalāsā: a title used for Sahaj-dhari (q.v.) Sikhs in the late eighteenth and early nineteenth centuries.

Khālistān: 'Land of the Pure', the name adopted by proponents of an independent homeland for the Sikhs.

Khālsā: the religious order established by Guru Gobind Singh in 1699.

Khatrī: a mercantile caste of the Punjab.

kes: uncut hair, worn as one of the Five Ks (q.v.).

Kes-dhārī: a Sikh who retains the *kes* (q.v.).

kirpān: sword or dagger, worn as one of the Five Ks (q.v.).

kīrtan: singing of gurbani (q.v.) or other hymns.

Kūkā Sikh: a member of the Namdhari sect of Sikhs (q.v.).

langar: the kitchen/refectory attached to every gurdwara from which food is served to all regardless of caste or creed; the meal served from such a kitchen.

mahant: the head of a religious establishment; incumbents of the gurdwaras until their disestablishment in 1925.

mañjī: administrative subdivision of the early Panth (q.v.).

masand: administrative deputy acting for the Guru.

Mazhabī: the Sikh section of the Chuhra or sweeper caste.

Mirāsī: a depressed sub-caste of Muslim genealogists and musicians, also called Dum or Dom.

mirī–pīrī: doctrine that the Guru possesses temporal (*mirī*) as well as spiritual authority (*pīrī*).

misl: a military cohort of the mid-eighteenth century Khalsa.

misldār: a lesser chieftain of a misl (under a sardar, q.v.).

Monā: a Sikh who cuts his/her hair.

mukti: liberation.

nakalī: spurious, false.

nām: the divine Name, a summary term expressing the total being of Akal Purakh (q.v.).

nām dān iśnān: the divine Name, charity, and either ablutions or pure living.

Nāmdhārī Sikh: member of the Namdhari Sikh sect (also known as Kuka Sikhs), followers of Balak Singh and Ram Singh.

nām japan: devoutly repeating the divine Name.

nām simaran: the devotional practice of meditating on the divine Name or *nām* (q.v.).

Nānak-panth: the community of Nanak's followers; the early Sikh community; (later) members of the Sikh community who do not observe the discipline of the Khalsa (q.v.).

Nāth tradition: yogic sect of considerable influence in the Punjab prior to and during the time of the early Sikh Gurus; practitioners of *hatha-yoga* (q.v.).

Nirankār: 'Without Form', a name of Akal Purakh (q.v.) used by Nanak.

Nirankārī Sikh: member of the Nirankari Sikh sect, follower of Baba Dayal (1783–1855) and his successors.

nirguṇa: 'without qualities', formless, non-incarnated (cf. *saguṇa*).

nit-nem: the Sikh daily liturgy.

paṅgat: '[sitting in] line', the custom whereby equality is maintained in the langar (q.v.).

pāhul: the Khalsa initiation ceremony, baptism.

pañj kakke, pañj kakār: the 'Five Ks'; the five items, each beginning with 'k', which members of the Khalsa must wear.

pañj mel: the five reprobate groups.

pañj piāre: the 'cherished five'; the first five Sikhs to be initiated as members of the Khalsa in 1699; five Sikhs in good standing chosen to represent a sangat (q.v.)

panth: 'path' or 'way', system of religious belief or practice, community observing particular system of belief or practice.

Panth: the Sikh community (*panth* spelt with a capital 'P').

panthic: concerning the Panth.

patit: 'fallen', apostate, renegade.

Patit, Patit Sikh: a Kes-dhari (q.v.) Sikh who cuts his hair; an initiated Sikh who has committed one of the four gross sins (the *chār kurahit*) (q.v.).

pīr: the head of a Sufi (q.v.) order; a Sufi saint; (loosely) a holy man, whatever his religion.

pīrī: the authority of a *pīr* (q.v.); spiritual authority.

pothī: tome, volume.

Purātan: one of the extant collections of janam-sakhi anecdotes.

qaum: 'a people who stand together'.

qāzī: a Muslim judge, administrator of Islamic law.

rāga: metrical mode.

Rahit: the code of conduct of the Khalsa (q.v.).

rahit-nāmā: a recorded version of the Rahit (q.v.).

rāj karegā khālsā: 'the Khalsa shall rule'.

Rāmgaṛhīā: a Sikh artisan caste, predominantly drawn from the Tarkhan (q.v.) or carpenter caste but also including Sikhs from the blacksmith, mason, and barber castes.

śabad (śabda): word; a hymn of the Adi Granth (q.v.).

sādh: a virtuous person; practitioner of Sant teachings (q.v.).

sādh sangat: the fellowship of the devout; congregation of the pious.

saguna: 'with qualities', possessing form (cf. *nirguṇa*).

sahaj: slow, easy, natural; the condition of ultimate, inexpressible beatitude, the condition of ineffable bliss resulting from the practice of *nām simaraṇ* (q.v.).

Sahaj-dhārī: a non-Khalsa Sikh.

sākhī: a section of a janam-sakhi (q.v.), normally an anecdote.

Sanātan Sikhs: conservative members of the Singh Sabha (q.v.).

saṅgat: congregation, group of devotees.

Sant: one who knows the truth; a pious person; an adherent of the Sant tradition (q.v.); one renowned as a teacher of Gurmat (q.v.).

Sant Khālsā: 'the divine Khalsa', a title used by the Namdhari Sikhs (q.v.) for the Khalsa (q.v.).

Sant tradition: a devotional tradition of north India which stressed the need for interior religion as opposed to external observance.

Sarbat Khālsā: 'the Entire Khalsa'; representative assembly of the Khalsa (q.v.).

sardār: the chief of a misl (q.v.); in modern usage the standard mode of address for all Kes-dhari male Sikhs.

Sati-nām: 'True is the Name'; '[Thy] Name is Truth'.

satsaṅg: assembly of true believers.

savā lakh: 125,000, the number whom a single member of the Khalsa equals in battle.

sevā: service, commonly to a gurdwara.

Shiromanī Akālī Dal: the Akali Party.

Shiromanī Gurdwārā Parbandhak Committee: the committee which controls the historic gurdwaras of the Punjab (commonly referred to as the SGPC).

Siṅgh Sabhā: Sikh movement founded in 1873 for the reform and regeneration of the Panth.

Sūfī: a member of one of the mystical orders of Islam.

takhat: 'throne'; one of the five centres of temporal authority.

tanakhāh: a penance for a violation of the Rahit (q.v.).

tanakhāhīā: a person who is guilty of a transgression against the Rahit (q.v.).

Tarkhān: the carpenter caste.

Tat Khālsā: the 'True Khalsa' or the 'Pure Khalsa'. In the early eighteenth century the immediate followers of Banda Bahadur. In the late nineteenth and twentieth centuries radical members of the Singh Sabha (q.v.).

Udāsī: adherent of the Udasi panth (q.v.), an order of ascetics (normally celibate) who claim as their founder Siri Chand (one of Guru Nanak's sons).

Vāhigurū: 'Praise to the Guru'; the modern name for God.

Vaiśnava, Vaishnava: believer in, practitioner of bhakti (q.v.) directed to the God Visnu.

vār: ode; a poetic form.

visamād: wonder, awe.

THE TEN GURUS

1. Guru Nanak (1469–1539)
2. Guru Angad (1504–52)
3. Guru Amar Das (1479–1574)
4. Guru Ram Das (1534–81)
5. Guru Arjan (1563–1606)
6. Guru Hargobind (1595–1644)
7. Guru Hari Rai (1630–61)
8. Guru Hari Krishan (1656–64)
9. Guru Tegh Bahadur (1621–75)
10. Guru Gobind Singh (1666–1708)

INDEX